™

Prima's Official Strategy Guide
Rick Barba

Prima Games
A Division of
Prima Communications, Inc.

3000 Lava Ridge Court
Roseville, CA 95661
(916) 787-7000
www.primagames.com

Project Editor: Jill Hinckley
Assistant Project Editor: Candace English
Editorial Assistant: Etelvina Hernandez
Product Manager: Jennifer Crotteau

ISBN: 7615-3087-8
Library of Congress Catalog Card Number: 00-10491
Printed in the United States of America

00 01 02 03 BB 10 9 8 7 6 5 4 3 2 1

Table of Contents

Foreword

Intelligence is an interesting thing. It's a fairly recent innovation in evolution, our ancestors having basically been pond scum for about 3 billion years beforehand. The ability to adapt more rapidly (than genetic evolution) to changing environments seems to be the basic reward of intelligence. The cost of this intelligence is balanced against many other factors, from rate of reproduction (rabbits) to body mass (birds).

But why did humans go so overboard? Our brains are almost too big at birth, our young are not self-sufficient for years, and we're physically not that impressive compared to many other animals.

There seems to be some evidence that our intelligence is the result of a vicious feedback cycle, a cycle that begins with social behavior. At some point in our history we began to compensate for our weaknesses by banding together in tribes and clans, much like wild primates. Our family structures became more stable. The social structures in these groups— and our ancestor's individual standing within them—became a larger and larger component of our environment over time. Basically our roles and behaviors in these societies started to become as complex as the rest of the outside world.

Perhaps, it is thought, this became a major impetus for the growth of our brain mass. We needed bigger brains to be successful in our own societies (which were helping us to become successful at the game of survival). We needed to understand clearly the needs, motivations, and intentions of our families, clan members, and competing humanoids. Most of the other high intelligence animals on Earth also seem to be highly social creatures (dolphins, chimpanzees).

As our intelligence progressed, we evolved and devised ever more elaborate means of communication, culminating in the development of symbolic grammars like math, language, and music. From the perspective of other species on Earth we are almost telepathic in our abilities to communicate complex ideas to one another.

Along our path we came up with many interesting tools that allowed us to not only shape our external world of wood, rocks and fire, but also our internal world of communication, planning, and symbols. One of these tools was the game. Many animals exhibit the more general aspects of play (as a learning mechanism, where they can experiment with survival strategies while young), but only humans have taken play into the purely symbolic realm of games (with well-defined rules and metaphors).

So it seems only appropriate (and somewhat ironic) that the reason we are so tuned into the thoughts, feelings and motivations of other people is because that is what has been growing our brains for the last million years or so. We have become so adept at modeling the mental state of others because our societies (and hence survival) depended on that ability.

Seems like a good excuse for a rather odd game, anyway.

—Will Wright

Introduction

In January of 2000 we braved the Y2K skies and sojourned to Walnut Creek, California for a privileged tour of *The Sims* conducted by none other than Will Wright himself. Indeed, over the course of our three-day visit, Will graciously lifted the lid of his software "dollhouse" (the original working title of the game) and shared its inner secrets with us.

Now we pass them on to you.

And that's the beauty of an official strategy guide, isn't it? The words go directly from the design gods into our tape recorder, then onto the page, and then to you. So here, in your hands right now, you hold an intimate map to all of the secret places in *The Sims* that only Will Wright and his EA/Maxis team of developers knew about until they spilled the beans onto our hungry little micro-cassette recorder.

And now we've repeated that process and gone back to the horse's mouth for the secrets of *The Sims: Livin' Large* expansion pack. Once again, you get the inside dope on stuff, including *Livin' Large*'s wild new interactive items—the crystal ball, the chemistry lab, the genie lamp, the telescope, the wonderful Vibromatic Heart Bed, and more. Want to cure the dreaded Guinea Pig Disease? *Read this book!*

Before we proceed, however, let us make one very important point: *This strategy guide begins where The Sims game manual ends.* In fact, we assume you've not only read the excellent manual but have played the game a bit and have a basic familiarity with its controls. If you have not explored the manual yet, please do so now. It's a pleasant read filled with indispensable information about navigating *The Sims*.

That said, this guide is structured to have something for every type of Sim fan. Each chapter features a comprehensive examination of the inner workings of *The Sims,* peering into the very depths of the engine programming in many cases. But that shouldn't scare off casual gamers. Each section builds from a general strategy overview and includes plenty of simple, straightforward tips in easy-to-find hint boxes.

Again, many of these tips come courtesy of the Maxis development team, including Will Wright himself, as do the dozens of point tables, graphs, charts, and other valuable game data you'll find in this book. Other nuggets of insight come from the *real* experts—the Electronic Arts testing team that crunched the game, day and night, for months on end. You'll find these gems in our "Tips from the Testers" sections liberally sprinkled throughout each chapter.

One last note: Be sure to check out the last section, "Creating Your Own Sim Stuff." It's remarkably easy to customize *The Sims* to model your own personal view of neighborhood life, no matter how unique or, OK, we'll say it, *perverse*. And take regular visits to the *The Sims* official website at http://www.thesims.com to "shop" for new catalog items for the game. (It's free, of course.)

Acknowledgments

The first acknowledgment goes to the obvious. Everybody now, say it with me: *Thank you, Mr. Wright.* My own thanks go to Will not only for his brilliant, addictive, non-violent, hands-down game of the year (if not the decade) . . . but also for his generous help and warm hospitality during my visit to Maxis.

Second, this book would not have been remotely possible without the attentive over-sight of Chris Trottier, associate producer for *The Sims*. Her patient review of early drafts and our daily e-mail exchanges kept things accurate and on track. And for the *Livin' Large* updates, my thanks to producer Chris Baena and assistant producer Sean Baity, who fed me all the new data with promptness and good humor.

Thanks also to software engineer Patrick J. Barrett III, who clarified and verified much of the information in this book, and to artist Eric Chin for providing graphic materials with amazing alacrity.

Last but not least, my deepest gratitude goes to the Electronic Arts testers who provided a wealth of helpful materials. Thanks to Andrew Blomquist, Syruss Flyte, Peter Trice, Ed O'Tey, and Jason Morales for their insightful tips (including the weird sadistic ones).

1
Cheats and Quick Start Tips

et's kick off our pre-game coverage with the inside scoop, the real reason you bought this strategy guide in the first place (admit it)—cheat codes. We managed to scam a comprehensive list of codes from the Maxis development team.

We also strong-armed the Electronic Arts quality-control testers into revealing a few of their sneaky "quick-start" tips—clever ways to maximize your bank account in the early going.

Oh, and we found that the game's only known Easter egg (as of this writing) is the product of programmer Patrick Barrett, who broke down and revealed it to us after a couple of minor stalking incidents: after you use the Help System in *The Sim*s for 100 days, it begins to give you info about design team members.

Thanks, Patrick. We'll be in touch.

Cheat Codes

To bring up the Cheat window, press [Ctrl][Shift][C]. Then key in the cheat code. Some cheat functions may seem arcane to the average player. Don't worry, they made us feel stupid, too. But hackers will probably find some useful tools for evading the NORAD detection 'bots.

This list of codes starts with the ones most people want first—the money cheats—plus one other we found pretty cool, the water tool cheat. The rest follow in alphabetical order.

rosebud

Adds 1,000 simoleans to your bank account. It also activates the ability to use the following cheat.

!;!;!;

Each "!;" (exclamation point/semicolon) pair adds 1,000 simoleans to your account. Must be activated by entering the previous "rosebud" cheat first.

water_tool

This cheat enables the water tool for land-scaping your lot with water. To deactivate the water tool, go into Build mode and pick another tool. Hold down [Ctrl] and use the left mouse button to recreate land. Remember that water blocks Sims routing.

Fig. 1-1. Add streams, ponds, and creepy bogs (like this one in the Goths' backyard cemetery) with the water tool cheat.

autonomy (0 to 100)

This cheat sets the autonomous behavior level of all the Sims in the house. Enter 0 to turn autonomy off, 50 to set it to normal level. Enter 100 for "super autonomy," which allows Sims to do things that only the users can do.

bubble_tweak (0 to –65)

This cheat sets the 'z' value to offset the Sims' thought bubbles. The default is –65, so the bubbles don't poke through the headboards on beds.

draw_all_frames (on/off)

Draw all animation frames without skipping to keep up. This allows you to view all animations but forces the game speed to zero at times.

draw_floorable (on/off)

Turns the floorable grid on and off in Build mode when you add a second story. It's defaulted to "on." ("Floorable" describes an area where you can place floor grids. Don't you love designer-speak?)

draw_routes (on/off)

Draw colored dots on the selected Sim's path. This one's kind of cool.

genable (various settings)

Use this cheat to turn the drawing of surfaces to screen on and off. We're not sure why anyone would want to turn stuff off, but here's the list:

genable default: Sets everything to default.

genable status: Shows current settings.

genable terrain (on/off): Enables/disables terrain drawing.

genable floors (on/off): Enables/disables floor drawing.

genable walls (on/off): Enables/disables wall drawing.

genable objects (on/off): Enables/disables object drawing.

genable people (on/off): Enables/disables people drawing.

genable all (on/off): Enables/disables all the foregoing.

grid (on/off)

Enables/disables terrain grid drawing.

grow_grass (amount)

Increases the grass level to the maximum for each tile. To turn brown grass to green on your lot, key in 150 as the amount.

history (file)

Writes the current family's history to a file. If the file is unspecified, the default is used. The default is *FamilyHistory.txt*, written to *The Sims* folder.

map_edit (on/off)

Use this cheat to lock and unlock floor tiles. You can't edit—that is, move objects, change terrain, build floors or walls, and so on—a locked tile. Such tiles usually lie at the edges of a lot. The mailbox and outside trash can lie on locked tiles, for example, as do the road and the border around the lot.

move_objects (on/off)

Turn this function on to move any object.

preview_anims (on/off)

Turns Animation Preview mode on and off. This function allows you to click on an object and view any selected Sim's animation for it. Why is this useful? It's a secret. Nobody can tell you.

rotation (0)

Sets a lot's rotation to its default, as seen from the Neighborhood screen.

route_balloons (on/off)

Defaulted off. Use this cheat to view a Sim's intermediate route balloon info.

sim_speed (speed)

This cheat alters the speed of the game. The range is from −1000 (a virtual crawl—kind of cool, like slo-mo) to 1000 (same as the Ultra Speed button on the Control Panel).

sim_log (begin/end)

Start and stop Sim logging. Writes a *SimLog.txt* file to *The Sims* folder.

Will Wright explains: "If you type 'sim_log begin' and play a while, the game will keep track of everything each character does. Typing 'sim_log end' stops and displays the text file.

"The file is a Tab-delimited text file that can easily be read into Microsoft Excel. The file includes a row of data for each interaction that's occurred, sorted by the object involved. This data includes routing time, interaction time, the change in each motive during interaction, and the character performing the interaction.

"We used this feature quite a lot during game tuning. I'm sure our players will figure out some really interesting things to do with this."

sweep (on/off/none)

Displays the in-game frame profiler. Click in the Sweep window and use your up/down arrow keys to change events being profiled, and your left/right arrow keys to adjust the milliseconds per tick.

You'll find this utility useful for running background checks on suspected Algerian terrorists, for example . . . .

tile_info (on/off)

Show or hide the Tile Info window: move the mouse over a tile, click in the Tile Info window, and then press R to view base object info.

New LIVIN' LARGE Neighborhoods

The *Livin' Large* expansion pack gives *The Sims* five "built-in" neighborhoods. Select new neighborhoods by using the arrow buttons in the upper-left corner of the Neighborhood screen. Neighborhood 1 is reserved for the existing neighborhood players created using *The Sims*. Neighborhood 2 contains houses made by Maxis for *Livin' Large*. Neighborhoods 3, 4, and 5 are empty.

Note, however, that you can maintain *more* than five neighborhoods in *Livin' Large*. First, open *The Sims* game directory. You should find five *UserData* folders; the first is unnumbered, the others numbered 2 to 5. Each holds the data for one of your five *Livin' Large* neighborhoods. You'll also find a folder named *TemplateUserData*. This holds all data for a blank new neighborhood.

Now take the following steps:

1. Make a copy of the *TemplateUserData* folder. One way is to hold down Ctrl and drag the folder to the desktop.
2. Rename this copy *UserData*[XX], where XX is a number between 6 and 99 unused by any of the other *UserData* folders.
3. Move this new *UserData*[XX] folder into *The Sims* directory with the other *UserData* folders.

You can do this before you run the game, or you can do it during the game by hitting [Alt][Tab] to go to the Windows desktop. Either way, *The Sims: Livin' Large* should register the fact that you added a new neighborhood.

Here's an example:

- You're running the game, and you decide you want to add a new neighborhood to hold some new families you recently imported from *www.TheSims.com*.

- You [Alt][Tab] to the Windows desktop, find the installation folder for *The Sims*—again, you must have the *Livin' Large* expansion pack installed—and make a copy of *TemplateUserData*.

- You rename this folder "UserData23."

- You [Alt][Tab] back to the game.

- As you scroll through the different neighborhoods, "23" shows up. This refers to your new *UserData23* directory.

- Now you can use the Import Family button (on the Neighborhood screen) to put the new families into this new Neighborhood 23.

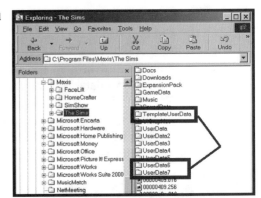

Fig. 1-2. To create new neighborhoods beyond the five in THE SIMS: LIVIN' LARGE, make a copy of the TEMPLATEUSERDATA folder, rename it USERDATA[6 to 99], and put it in THE SIMS directory.

Quick Start Tips

We harassed Electronic Arts testers Syruss Flyte and Andrew Blomquist into revealing some of the Fraternity of Testers' most intimate secrets for building cash quickly in *The Sims*. Here are a few of the more effective (and nefarious) tactics.

The Bob and Betty Cheat

If you've played the tutorial, you know Bob and Betty Newbie. This delightful couple provides a nice, safe introduction to *The Sims* because (as we learned by snooping through Will Wright's desk) the game's Motive engine mutes the usual degradation of their needs until you complete the tutorial.

In other words, neither Bob's nor Betty's needs drop very fast while the tutorial is active. Most, in fact, won't drop at all.

Fig. 1-3. THE SIMS tutorial, starring Bob and Betty Newbie, gives you sneaky ways to build a nest egg quickly.

So here's a tip from EA tester Syruss Flyte: After Betty Newbie appears, ignore the tutorial directions for a while. Instead, get jobs for the Newbies, buy the espresso machine, put the game on Ultra Speed, and focus entirely on raising Bob's and Betty's skills.

The Hunger motive is frozen, so they won't need to eat. And, although they'll lose Energy at work and while exercising to increase their Body skill, they can recover by using the espresso machine five or six times instead of sleeping.

"In a relatively short time, Bob and Betty can max out all six of their skills," Flyte says.

After that, the super-Newbies move with alacrity up the ladder of success as they make more friends.

Fig. 1-4. Here's the ultimate Newbie skill-building room—piano (Creativity), bookshelf (Cooking and Mechanical), mirror (Charisma), chessboard (Logic), and exercise machine (Body). Use the espresso machine on the desk to replenish Energy.

EA tester Andrew Blomquist adds, "After you get jobs for Bob and Betty and build up all their skills, just let the game run on Ultra Speed. Walk away. In fact, let it sit overnight. In the morning your Newbies will be stinking rich."

Then you can finish the tutorial, create your own Sim family, kill off either Bob or Betty, and have one of your own Sims marry the surviving Newbie to bring his or her money-making skills *and* the entire Newbie estate into your household.

"If you're feeling particularly cold-blooded," adds Blomquist, "kill off the Newbie you married and keep the money for your Sim widow or widower." Then marry someone you like better. Isn't this fun?

But remember, one of these maxed-out Newbies can be the workhorse of your family, getting quick promotions with big paychecks, and bonuses, and other good stuff.

As you can see, game testers are Machiavellian. Of course, you'd be amoral, too, if you spent all day chained in a dark pit.

TIP

In *The Sims*, the houses are the saved games. Whenever you quit or return to the Neighborhood screen, you can save the changes to the house and its inhabitants. If you don't like the chain of events since you last saved, choose not to save, and then reenter the house from the Neighborhood screen.

The Slave Labor Method

Low-level jobs don't pay well, but it's the only employment you can find early in the game. The more workers you have bringing home paychecks at that time, the better.

Andrew Blomquist suggests you start a full-house "family" of eight Sim adults with the bare essentials for survival. Start seven Sims working right away and keep one poor slob home to keep house. Focus on the key survival motives—Hunger and Energy—but keep at least three of your folks in a good enough mood to advance their careers.

"You can just kill off the extra workers later," Blomquist adds coldly, "when the careers of your primary Sims stabilize and you have the equipment you need to get their motives up quickly and work on skills."

Fellow tester Syruss Flyte takes a slightly different approach to this method. Again, he suggests starting a family of eight Sim adults and putting them on an empty lot. Don't build anything, just place a good refrigerator. Then get each Sim a job. The best way to do this is to buy a cheap desk, computer, and chair. (Otherwise they all fight over the newspaper.)

Now run in Ultra Speed. This can be tricky. Your Sims will develop foul moods and fall asleep on the ground, so you have to make sure they go to work each day.

"But no matter how bad a mood your Sims develop, they never lose their jobs as long as you get them to their car pool," says Flyte. "With eight Sims working, you'll earn between §800 and §2,000 a day and, with only a fridge on the lot, the bills will be very low. Doesn't take long to build up a sizeable bank account."

You've got to admire the way Syruss thinks.

Marriage for Fun and Profit

This truly underhanded trick also comes courtesy of Syruss Flyte:

Create your family and move them onto a lot, but don't give them jobs. (Believe me, they won't have time to work with all the wooing that lies ahead.) Next, create a bunch of one-Sim "families," maxing out each Sim's personality with Nice and Outgoing points. Then move one of these single-Sim families into each remaining empty lot in the neighborhood. Give each lone Sim a small end table, a phone—and absolutely nothing else. Return to your family.

Now your family's entire focus is to meet, greet, befriend, flirt, and eventually marry every one of the lone Sim neighbors on the block. (Or, if the neighbors are the same sex, to convince them to join your household.)

Sure, you'll leave a trail of jealousy and broken hearts. But the payoff is big. Remember, whenever you marry the last adult Sim from another household, you gain not only a mate but also his or her entire net worth. In this case, each consummation brings your family almost §20,000 a pop. That adds up to a lot of simoleans.

The Big Box Method

Here's one last (and somewhat less extreme) startup trick from tester Andrew Blomquist. He suggests you can save a lot of money by not building interior walls at first.

"Walls cost money," he says, "and they increase the time it takes to route between objects." Indeed, walls are truly necessary only for bathroom privacy and to keep disturbances from awakening your sleeping Sims.

Blomquist says the best tactic is to build a simple one-by-two-tile room for both toilet and telephone. This gives you bathroom privacy and muffles the ringing phone. With the money you save, you can buy better objects for your Sims until money is no longer an issue.

Fig. 1-6. Put one nice, outgoing Sim on every lot with just a cheap end table and a phone. (We named this guy Rich Wedbait. Get it?) Return to your household, then have your family meet, woo, and marry all these affable Sims to get their assets.

Other Quick Tips

Here are some less tricky, more straightforward ways to get on the right track early. These tried and true methods come courtesy of our resident staff of Prima gaming experts.

Keep Things Manageable at First

A good starter family has just two adults, one with high Outgoing and Nice traits. Keep your nice, outgoing Sim at home doing housework, preparing meals, and making friends in the neighborhood. Send the other Sim to work. This way, meeting the family friend requirement for job promotions is no sweat for the working Sim, thanks to the stay-at-home partner.

Be a Good House Spouse and Get up Early

Stay-at-home Sims should wake an hour or two before their working partners and prepare a group meal—that is, select "Serve [Name of Meal]"—so the partners get as much rest as possible.

Stay-at-Home Partners Should Spend Time Reading Books on Cooking and Mechanical Topics

High Cooking skill boosts the Hunger satisfaction of meals prepared on stoves and in ovens and microwaves. Plus, it reduces the possibility of fire disasters. High Mechanical skill lets you fix plumbing and appliances yourself, avoiding the cost of hiring a Repairman. So when stay-at-home partners aren't tidying up or making friends, they should be hitting the bookshelf, hard.

Other Sims Are Entertaining . . . and Cheap

People are better than toys—at first, anyway. In the early going, save money by having Sims entertain one another to boost their Fun scores, instead of buying expensive toys and electronics. This boosts both Fun *and* Social scores. It also builds the Relationship score between the two Sims involved in the exchange.

Build Skills Before Job Seeking

The "Bob and Betty Cheat" mentioned earlier is a version of this basic starter tactic, but it can apply to all new Sim households. Build a very modest home and buy the barest minimum of amenities to save money. Don't take jobs right away. Instead, have Sims spend all their spare time building skills for several days, until their bankroll gets low. Building skills takes time, but it accelerates job promotions.

Skip Work Regularly to Spend Entire Days on Skill-Building Activities

Sims get fired only if they miss work two days in a row. So take days off regularly. In fact, consider working only every other day at first. Spend the off days building the skills that most apply to your chosen career. (If you're not sure which skills to build, check the tables in "The 15 Career Tracks" in chapter 6, "Careers and Skills.")

You miss out on some pay, but it's worth it because you gain salary-boosting promotions faster. Remember, skipping work has no effect on your job performance rating—unless, of course, you skip two days in a row.

2
Personality

When you first jumped into *The Sims*, you probably moved one of the game's premade families into the neighborhood. (If you're a guy, admit it—you went for the Roomies.) Then, of course, you got the itch to create your own Sims. When you create your own Sim family, you select their heads, bodies, and—wonder of wonders—their *personality traits*.

In this section, we examine how personality traits affect Sim behavior. We also look at some of the various preconfigured personality types—the zodiac signs—and see how they get along (or don't). Finally, we note a couple of amusing personality modifiers introduced in the *Livin' Large* expansion pack.

How Personality Affects Sim Behavior

When you construct a Sim, you assign points to five personality traits—Neat, Outgoing, Active, Playful, and Nice—in the Create a Sim screen. Changing the totals for these traits changes your Sim's attraction to certain activities and to other Sim types. For example, as the manual notes, a playful Sim is more likely to be drawn to a pinball machine than to a bookshelf.

Assigning points from 0 to 10 for each trait is like moving a slider bar between opposites. At 0 points, your Sim actually manifests the *opposite* of a particular trait. Thus, there are really 10 personality traits in *The Sims*, set up as pairs of opposites. They are:

- Neat/Messy
- Outgoing/Shy
- Active/Lazy
- Playful/Serious
- Nice/Grouchy

Fig. 2-1. Each personality trait encompasses both itself and its opposite. Here, Gozer is high on Neat and Outgoing, but is Lazy (low Active), Serious (low Playful), and Grouchy (low Nice).

Smooth-running Sim households often mix Sims with different traits for an efficient division of labor—a neatnik housekeeper, a nice and outgoing friend-maker, and so forth. Let's take a look at the activities associated with each personality trait.

Tips from the Testers

Choose your personalities to fit the roles you want your Sims to play. Neat Sims make very good stay-at-home cleaners. Outgoing and Nice helps a Sim looking to make family friends. Playful makes the Entertain and Joke interactions more readily available. Active Sims keep on the go and don't get uncomfortable easily.

—Peter Trice, Tester

Neat/Messy

Cleaning activities reach out and grab neat Sims. Neatniks are more likely to autonomously empty the trash, sweep up ash, mop up spills, clean up after meals, make beds, water flowers, bathe, wash hands, brush teeth, flush and clean toilets, clean tubs and showers, wind the old grandfather clock, and turn off the computer.

In fact, the following actions "push" to the front of the queue, based on your Sim's Neat rating. (For more on this, see the "Push" section in chapter 4, "Sim Autonomy," later in the book.)

On their own, neat Sims will:

- Wash their hands after eating pizza
- Flush and wash their hands after using the toilet
- Wash their hands after cleaning the toilet
- Make the bed after waking up

Messy Sims will:

- Create a puddle when getting out of the shower or bathtub
- Create a puddle when cleaning the aquarium
- Throw trash on the floor after eating a snack
- Leave a dirty plate after a meal

Fig. 2-2. Sims with high Neat points make swell stay-at-home housekeepers.

Outgoing/Shy

Outgoing Sims are people who need people. The Social motive score drops faster for them, so they need to spend more time socializing. Outgoing Sims have more social options. For example, they're more likely to dance, flirt, give backrubs, hug, entertain, compliment, brag, and tickle. They also respond more positively to these social interactions than shy people do. They have no compunction about joining others in games, dance, or the hot tub. Finally, they get more fun out of watching Romance on TV.

Fig. 2-3. Outgoing Sims enjoy backrubs and other highly social give-and-take activities. They're also more likely to join a group activity.

Shy people, on the other hand, prefer more solitary fun. Less outgoing folks would rather play in a fountain, and they're less likely to accept a hug or a backrub from another Sim. Shy Sims do need social interaction from time to time, however.

Fig. 2-4. Shy Sims (with low Outgoing points) prefer simpler interactions, such as playing in the fountain.

Tips from the Testers

I recommend always maxing out Outgoing and Nice attributes. The social aspect is extremely difficult without these stats—and practically impossible in cases where there are no Outgoing and Nice points allocated to a Sim's personality. With Nice and Outgoing maxed out, your Sim can often build a relationship to 100 the first time he or she meets a visiting Sim.

—Andrew Blomquist, Tester

Top Secret Hot Tub Tip

Here's a little detail *everybody* will be asking about. Only *you* will know the answer, though, because you were savvy enough to buy this strategy guide. Our inside source is none other than Will Wright.

Will says, "If the first Sim to get into your hot tub has a high Outgoing rating (7 or above), he or she climbs in naked; otherwise, he or she wears a swimsuit. Anyone who enters the hot tub after that wears whatever the first person did."

Active/Lazy

Sims with high Active ratings are drawn to activities such as shooting hoops, swimming in the backyard pool, and dancing at the stereo. Active Sim kids love to play on the outdoor play structure. And Active Sims naturally have the most fun watching Action shows on TV.

The Comfort motive score drops faster for lazy Sims. Thus, they should spend more quality time just sitting around. Lazy folks are more likely to nap in recliners or on sofas, watch TV, or soak in a hot tub. Wakeup time is longer for the lazy Sim, too, whereas active Sims practically leap out of bed.

Playful/Serious

Playful Sims have more social options than serious Sims do. They're more likely to entertain, joke, tickle, or scare other Sims, and they also respond more positively to such interactions. Playful Sims like to play with a baby, dollhouse, or computer game, shoot a game of pool, or fire up the pinball machine. They may even get a kick out of gazing at the goofy lawn flamingo. Playful Sim kids love to join in games of tag, scramble around on the backyard play structure, and play with toy boxes and train sets.

At the other end of the scale, more serious types would rather read a book or newspaper, play chess, or view a painting or sculpture.

NOTE

Although Sim kids inherit their individual personalities from their parents, in general they value fun more than adults.

Fig. 2-5. Playful Sims love games, jokes, tickling, and other high-spirited interactions. Kids, in particular, love fun activities.

Fig. 2-6. Serious Sims prefer to cozy up with a book or a quiet game of chess. They also have a higher appreciation of art objects.

Nice/Grouchy

Sims at the high end of the Nice scale are more likely to cheer up a moody friend or give a backrub, gift, or compliment. Nice Sims also like to tuck in their kids. Now, isn't that nice?

Sims at the Grouchy end of the scale are more inclined to brag, insult, slap, scare, or even attack other Sims. Grouchy Sims may even take a perverse pleasure in kicking a lawn flamingo or stomping on garden flowers.

Fig. 2-7. What could satisfy a grouchy Sim more than kicking a stupid lawn flamingo?

Fig. 2-8. The more playful your Sims, the more Fun points they can earn engaging in Fun activities.

How Personality Affects Fun

Interacting with certain objects can increase a Sim's Fun score. Although each object's point increase has a limit, certain personality traits raise the maximum Fun points a Sim can earn by as many as 10. To learn more about motive max, see "The Max (Motive) Factor" in chapter 3, "Mood and Motives."

TRAITS THAT RAISE MAX FUN VALUE

PERSONALITY TRAIT	RAISES MAX FUN SCORE FOR
Playful	Aquarium, Chess Table, Computer, Doll House, Flamingo, Pinball, TV (Cartoon Channel), VR Glasses
Serious (Low Playful)	Newspaper (Read)
Active	Basketball Hoop, Play Structure, TV (Action Channel)
Outgoing	Hot Tub, TV (Romance Channel)
Grouchy (Low Nice)	TV (Horror Channel)

How Personality Affects Skill Building

Sims can't advance in their world without increasing certain skills. They do so by using "skill-building" objects. Good news! Some personality traits accelerate the speed with which they acquire some skills.

Fig. 2-9. Outgoing Sims can build Charisma skill (by practicing speeches at mirrors) faster than shy Sims can.

SKILLS ACCELERATED BY PERSONALITY

SKILL	OBJECTS USED TO INCREASE SKILL	TRAIT ACCELERATOR
Creativity	Easel, Piano	Playful
Body	Exercise Machine, Swimming Pool	Active
Charisma	Medicine Cabinet, Mirrors	Outgoing
Mechanical	Woodworking Bench	Shy, Grouchy

Sim Zodiac Signs

When you assign points to the five Personality traits, you also create a zodiac sign for your Sim. Each zodiac sign also has a preconfigured trait "prototype." Will Wright and his team created these, and then tested every possible combination extensively to determine which signs got along best. The following table shows the results.

Fig. 2-10. Click on Personality, and then on a zodiac sign, to learn which signs your Sim is most or least compatible with.

Sim Zodiac Signs

Sign	Attracted To	Repelled By
Virgo	Aquarius/Sagittarius	Leo/Taurus
Libra	Virgo/Cancer	Pisces/Scorpio
Scorpio	Pisces/Leo	Libra/Aquarius
Sagittarius	Pisces/Capricorn	Libra/Scorpio
Leo	Sagittarius/Cancer	Capricorn/Gemini
Capricorn	Aquarius/Taurus	Leo/Gemini
Aquarius	Capricorn/Sagittarius	Scorpio/Virgo
Pisces	Scorpio/Gemini	Leo/Aries
Aries	Gemini/Taurus	Cancer/Libra
Taurus	Aries/Libra	Virgo/Cancer
Gemini	Pisces/Virgo	Capricorn/Aries
Cancer	Taurus/Scorpio	Gemini/Aries

> **NOTE**
> When creating a character, you can click on the zodiac to cycle through the different signs. It will automatically set the personality traits to reflect that sign.

How to Modify Personality: Crystal Ball and Chemistry Lab

After you create a Sim's personality (allocating points to Neat, Outgoing, etc.) on the Create a Sim screen and click Done, and then click Done in the Create a Family screen, the personality traits are locked—you cannot go back to the Create a Sim screen and edit them. However, the *Livin' Large* expansion pack includes a couple of fun items that can alter your Sim's personality.

The Crystal Ball

Here's the only real personality "cheat" in the game. The *Livin' Large* expansion pack adds the Madame Blahbatfry Crystal Ball (§760) to your catalog of Sim consumables. The item's description hints at its possible impact: "Look deep into the crystal ball . . . and then look deep into yourself . . . to start a journey of self-discovery and enhancement."

Once (and only once) each day, any adult Sim can "gaze" into the Madame Blahbatfry Crystal Ball to find a cryptic riddle referring to a particular personality trait. If you interpret the riddle correctly, then take certain actions to "exhibit" that trait, you gain a point of that trait.

For a complete rundown, see "How the Crystal Ball Works" in chapter 9, "Sim Objects." But here's a quick example. Your Sim gazes into the ball and gets a message

Madame Blahbatfry Crystal Ball

Some manners can only be taught
Some think these can be bought
If you are uncouth and unkind
You may soon come to find
Your niceness has come to naught.

[OK]

Fig. 2-11. The crystal ball can add trait points to your personality. Read the riddle, decipher the trait it refers to, and decide what actions might boost that trait.

that reads, "Those who lack will, soon become still. Those who are moving, find things improving." This riddle refers to the Sim's Active trait, challenging your Sim to keep active and moving. For the next Sim Day, the game monitors that Sim's Comfort motive. If the Comfort level goes down during the test period, indicating lots of movement and activity, the game adds one Active trait point to the Sim's personality. If the Comfort level goes up, however, the Sim *loses* an Active trait point.

The Chemistry Lab

Any adult Sim can use the "Concatenation Station" Home Chemistry Lab to create one of eight different colored potions, each with a different effect. The yellow potion induces a total "personality inversion" in any adult Sim who drinks it—that is, it sets all personality traits to their opposite.

For example, if you have a grouchy, serious, neat Sim—let's say Nice 2, Playful 3, Neat 10—the yellow potion turns him into a nice, playful slob with Nice 8, Playful 7, Neat 0. For detailed info on how the other chemistry lab potions affect your Sims, see "How the Chemistry Lab Works" in chapter 9, "Sim Objects."

Fig. 2-12. Knocking back a yellow potion induces a complete "personality inversion."

3

Mood and Motives

A s *The Sims* manual tells you, green Mood bars indicate a good mood (a state of happiness), and red Mood bars indicate a bad mood. Then, with tongue firmly in cheek, it suggests that each Sim's disposition reflects "a concatenation of various mood conditions and attributes, filtered through a fiendishly complicated computing formula reflecting the grandiose sophistication of the game."

Fig. 3-1. To keep your Sims happy, monitor their needs closely in the Control Panel's Mood display.

But, of course, any self-respecting strategy guide must peek under the hood at the Engine. So we made our way to Maxis in Walnut Creek, California, to meet with Will Wright and dig up some inside info.

Guess what? His computing formulas are fiendishly complicated.

The Motive Engine

Let's start with a quick review:

- Eight basic needs, or "motives"—Hunger, Comfort, Hygiene, Bladder, Energy, Fun, Social, and Room—drive each Sim.

- Each motive displays as a horizontal color bar depicting a scale of 200 points, from 100 (totally fulfilled need) at far right to –100 (totally unfulfilled need) at far left.

- When the motive is above zero, the color bar is green.

- When the motive is less than zero, the color bar is red.

- When a motive drops very low, it's time to attend to that particular need.

How Mood Is Calculated

The Motive Engine averages the motives' eight scores to calculate your Sim's Mood rating. But it's not a simple average. It's a *weighted* average: that is, each motive carries more or less weight, depending on how high or low it is. For example, a very low Hunger score puts a Sim on the verge of death. So naturally, the lower the Hunger score drops, the more weight it carries in the Mood calculation.

TIP

Physical needs gain considerable weight the lower they drop. Very low Hunger, Bladder, or Comfort scores can lower the overall Mood score considerably. Sometimes a simple meal, a trip to the toilet, or a rest in a comfy chair can raise a Sim's Mood several bars higher.

Makes sense, doesn't it? Even with all your other needs (Fun, Social, etc.) maxed out in the green, your own mood would be pretty low if you were starving. The same is true of the Bladder motive: the greater *anybody's* Bladder need, the greater its weight in the mood calculation.

Fig. 3-2. The Mood bars reflect a "weighted average" of all other needs. Each bar represents a 20-point increment on the Mood scale from −100 to 100.

The "Happy Weights" Charts

Caution: Stop here if numbers hurt you! Believe me, casual players certainly know all they need to know about how a Sim's mood is determined. Again, the basic concept is this: the lower or higher a motive score is, the more weight it carries in the game's mood calculation. Scores associated with physical needs—Hunger primarily, but also Comfort and Bladder—are weighted heavier than others as they plunge lower into the red. On the other hand, a Social score of 100 can have a dramatic effect on mood as well.

But all you number-crunchers and engine-tinkerers, follow us in. A Sim's Mood score, as mentioned, is calculated as a weighted average of that Sim's eight motive scores. Specifically, this means each of the eight motive scores is multiplied by a value (thus, "weighted") that corresponds to how high or low that motive score is at the moment. After these multipliers have modified all eight motive scores, they're averaged to calculate the Mood score. (To see how the Mood point score translates into the 10 Mood bars, refer to Figure 3-2.)

The following graphs depict the multipliers (weights) used in the mood calculation for two very different motives, Hunger and Fun. Again, physical needs such as Hunger,

Comfort, and Bladder carry the most weight when their scores get low. On the other hand, Fun and Social considerations gain weight as the overall Mood score rises.

Again, it makes sense, doesn't it?

As you can see, the lower a Sim's Hunger score, the higher the multiplier. Indeed, the upward curve is quite steep as the Sim approaches the starvation score of –100. As Hunger drops from –60 to –100, the multiplier shoots up from 5 to 15! So when a Sim's Hunger score hits, say, –99 (moments before grisly death), the mood calculation multiplies –99 times 14.75 when averaging the motive scores.

That's lot of negative points to average in. Thus, you can see how weighted it is, and how being really hungry drags a Sim's mood right down into the red.

On the other hand, as Hunger and Fun motive scores increase, the weight, or multiplier, for Fun grows more important. In fact, at higher motive scores, Fun carries from three to five times more weight than Hunger. (The Hunger weight stays at 1 after the Hunger motive score crosses zero into the green region.) Again, when your belly is full, you forget about food and think about fun.

A Sim's Eight Basic Needs

Yes, Sims have eight needs. They satisfy these needs by interacting with objects or other Sims. As a rule, consult the ratings in the game's Buy mode catalog to see how well a given object will satisfy a given need. The higher the rating, the better the object will satisfy the motive (need) listed.

Fig. 3-3. Check the Buy mode catalog to learn which objects boost which motives. This model railroad is fun, enhances the room, and attracts a crowd.

The Max [Motive] Factor

But not only do different objects increase motives at different speeds, many objects can bring only the motive they satisfy to a certain maximum value. When your Sims hit this "Max [Motive]" value, they disengage from the activity (except in a few special skill-building activities). This Max [Motive] factor is why Sims sometimes don't take wholeheartedly to the activities you select for them.

Motive Decay

Motives, of course, decay over time, creating increasingly dire needs. We'll discuss the various motives in more depth later in the chapter. For now, read on for some quick tips on how motive decay works.

- Most motives decay more slowly while Sims sleep or work.
- Comfort decays more quickly for Lazy (low Active) people.

- Social decays more quickly for Outgoing people.
- Energy decays at a constant rate, except when strenuous physical activity accelerates it.
- Bladder decays at a constant rate, except when food or beverage consumption stimulates it.
- Hunger decay slows considerably as the Hunger score approaches the bottom of the scale.
- Fun decays more quickly for kids.

Hunger: The Food Chain Revealed

Hunger is the primal need, the one at the bottom of Maslow's pyramid, the foundation of all other needs, the one you can least afford to ignore. Much of real life is organized around the regular consumption of food. Life in *The Sims* is no different. So here's a step-by-step look at what the Maxis design team calls the "food chain."

First, Get a Refrigerator

In *The Sims*, the food chain starts at the refrigerator. Basically, without a fridge, your Sims have very few food options—Pizza and Grilling. Subsisting on pizza might not sound so bad at first. But really—pizza for every meal? Scary. And pizza is expensive, too. At §40 a pie, it adds up, costing far more than a fridge over time. And you have to wait an hour for delivery. And deal with Freddy the Pizza Dude.

Hey, get a refrigerator. First thing. Trust us on this one.

Fig. 3-4. The food chain in THE SIMS starts at the refrigerator. Without a fridge, your only food option is pizza delivery.

TIP

If your Sim raids the fridge and ends up eating a can of beans, you have no food prep area available. Sims prepare far more nourishing meals on an open counter or in a food processor.

Food Prep

Once your Sim gets a fridge and grabs ingredients for a meal, the next link in the food chain is the food prep area. Sims can prepare food in only two places—on a counter or in a food processor. Sims won't use tables or desks for food prep. Nor will they prepare food on counters cluttered with other stuff—dirty plates, pizza boxes, newspapers, piles of bills, or other appliances, such as coffeemakers. If no food prep area is available, your Sim stands in the kitchen with great pathos, eating cold beans from a can.

Counters

First, all counters are created equal. Upgrading to expensive counters does not enhance the food prep process in any way, so counter-buying is an aesthetic choice and nothing else. Using any counter for food prep adds 16 points to the meal's Hunger motive.

All counters have equal effect on the time it takes to prepare the food, too. Only Cooking skill affects meal prep time.

Food Processors

Food processors prepare more satisfying meals than do counters because they add 32 points to the meal's Hunger motive—twice the increase of countertop food prep. They also prepare food faster than you would be able to on a counter. As with counters, prep time is modified by Cooking skill.

XLR8R Food Processor $220
Part of the Intelli-kitchen total food prep system, the XLR8R accelerates food delivery time...AND taste. The low-cost, high-precision pulse-echo radar blades enable invariable food chunk tolerances by combining digital logic with microwave techniques. Sealed housing. Quick lock lid. Finger Shield. Idi-Pruuf control panel.
Hunger: 2

Fig. 3-5. Counters are fine for prep work, but the trusty XLR8R Food Processor adds more to your meal.

Cooking Appliances

OK, you've prepped the food. Now what? Naturally, your Sim looks for someplace to cook it. Sims can cook food in the toaster oven, microwave, or on one of four stoves. (The original version of *The Sims* features just two stoves, but the *Livin' Large* expansion pack adds two more.) Both the microwave and the toaster oven take the same amount of time to cook your meal. If your Sim finds no cooking appliance—well, enjoy your salad, pal—or the Quick Meal equivalent, a Box o' Cold Yuck. Note that when you cook a meal, your Sim's Cooking skill affects both cooking time and Hunger point increase.

> **NOTE**
>
> In a pinch, your Sim can prepare meals atop dishwashers or trash compactors. Each of these items adds only 5 points to the meal's Hunger score increase, however.

> **TIP**
>
> When Sims cook meals, more expensive appliances provide greater Hunger satisfaction. Also, the higher your Sim's Cooking skill, the faster and more satisfying the meal.

Stoves

The four stove models include the Dialectric free-standing range (adds 32 points to the meal's Hunger motive), the Pyrotorre gas range (adds 40 points), the

CiaoTime 360 Moderna cooktop (adds 48 points), and the Olde Thyme Restored Oven (adds 55 points). Additionally, each stove adds the following to the Hunger motive: $1.5 \times$ Cooking skill.

Careful, though. Low-skill cooks stand a good chance of starting a cooking fire. (See "Fire, Theft, and Accidents" in chapter 7, "Sim Economics 101.")

Toaster Oven

The wonderfully cheap Brand Name toaster oven is worth a mere nine Hunger points to your meal. Add to that your Sim's current Cooking skill to determine your meal's total Hunger motive increase. Poor cooks can start a fire with ease using this baby. Every meal cooked in the toaster oven takes the same amount of time—five game minutes.

Fig. 3-6. The top-of-the-line Old Thyme Restored Oven adds a hefty 55 Hunger points to any cooked meal.

Microwave

The Positive Potential microwave uses its "neo-non-ionizing radiation in a magnetron tube to enable half-wave voltage octupling." And that means good food! This glowing technology zaps 16 points into the meal; add your Sim's Cooking skill to determine its total Hunger motive increase. Sims won't start fires with the microwave, although they may irradiate much of the tri-state area.

Barbecue Grill

The Wild Bill THX-451 barbecue is a special part of the food chain. Burgers start and end here. Its single available interaction, "Grill," includes the prep and cooking of a group platter of six meals. Grilling adds 16 points to the Hunger motive increase for each barbecued meal.

Any cook can start a BBQ fire; Cooking skill is irrelevant. The proximity of other objects triggers fire risk.

How Appliances and Food Prep Surfaces Affect Hunger Score

As the foregoing descriptions demonstrate, each prep surface or appliance adds points to the meal's Hunger motive. We gathered all those values into a single table because, well, that's the type of guys we are.

HOW APPLIANCES AND SURFACES AFFECT HUNGER SCORE

APPLIANCE/SURFACE	HUNGER POINTS ADDED TO MEAL
Fridge (Llamark)	9
Fridge (Porcina)	12
Fridge (Freeze Secret)	16
Fridge (Old Thyme)	18
All Counters (NuMica, Tiled, Cornerstone, Barcelona)	16
Food Processor	32
Dishwasher	5
Trash Compactor	5
Stove (Dialectric)	32 (plus 1.5 x Cooking skill)
Stove (Pyrotorre)	40 (plus 1.5 x Cooking skill)
Stove (CiaoTime)	48 (plus 1.5 x Cooking skill)
Stove (Old Thyme)	55 (plus 1.5 x Cooking skill)
Microwave	16 (plus Cooking skill)
Toaster Oven	9 (plus Cooking skill)

Food

OK, time to gorge—on food data, that is. Here's where you learn everything about food items in *The Sims*—cost, types, Hunger points, spoilage rates, and other succulent tidbits of information.

Cost of Meals

Five meal types cost money in *The Sims*.

- Snack: §5
- Meal: §10
- Group Meal: §20
- Barbecue Meal: §20
- Pizza: §40

Hunger Score for Each Meal

In addition to all the Hunger motive points various prep and cooking methods add, each meal type has its own Hunger point value.

MEAL TYPE	HUNGER MOTIVE POINTS
Snack	9
Quick Meal	16
Full Meal	16
Group Meal (Per Serving)	16
Pizza (Per Serving)	33
Robo-Food (Per Serving)	33

Food Types

The Sims offers a surprising variety of foods for your munching pleasure. The same meal type can manifest several ways, depending on food prep (or lack thereof) and cooking appliance (or lack thereof). And not all food in *The Sims* is a "meal." Fridge snacks and food gifts from visitors (candy or fruitcakes) add Hunger points, too. Here's a quick rundown of all the game's food types.

Pizza

Ah, pizza. Favored food of game designers and Q & A testers everywhere. In *The Sims*, the only source of pizza is Freddy the Pizza Dude. To order, simply pick up the phone and, under Services, select Pizza. Freddy arrives with your §40 pie within the hour. Six slices of pizza come in each box. Pizza offers a stout 33 Hunger points per slice. (This may seem like a lot, but remember that pizza servings aren't enhanced, point-wise, by prep and cooking.) Once delivered, the pizza box can be placed on the ground. But Sims only eat while standing. Neat Sims wash their hands after a greasy pizza-fest.

Fig. 3-7. Pizza hits the spot when you don't have time to cook. Here, the gals chow down and chat about soccer.

Robo-Food

The *Livin' Large* expansion pack adds a home robot named Servo, a true homeowner's dream. As the catalog description puts it: "Your lack of respect for the dignity of work gives Servo a reason to live!" He cleans, kills roach infestations, does gardening, repairs broken stuff, and serves wonderful group meals (with six servings). These meals boost your Hunger score by 33 points per serving, same as a serving of pizza.

For more info on Servo, find "Servo" in the "List of Object Interactions" in chapter 9, "Sim Objects."

NOTE

Servo can only prepare and serve a meal if no other edible meal exists in the active Sim household.

TIP

Pizza, as you might expect, is good party food. Visitors can stand and chat pleasantly while eating. This applies to all meals eaten with another person. (For more on this type of interaction, see "Group Talk" in chapter 5, "Social Interactions.")

Have Snack

Snacks come directly from the refrigerator, require no prep or cooking, and give a quick (if small) burst of Hunger satisfaction. Sims grab a snack from the fridge and eat it right away, while standing. Each snack offers nine Hunger points by itself; include the points offered by the refrigerator model to determine total Hunger motive increase.

Have Quick Breakfast/Lunch/Dinner

This light meal is taken from the fridge as a closed box and requires no prep. Your Sim either cooks it or, if no cooking appliance is available, stands and eats right from the box. If cooked, the Quick Meal may be eaten sitting or standing. The Hunger motive increase is 16 points plus the points added by the refrigerator model and (if any) the cooking device.

Fig. 3-8. Snacks are good for a quick Hunger fix. Kids can't cook, but they can help themselves to snacks.

Have Breakfast/Lunch/Dinner

This is a full, single meal. Depending on prep and cooking, it can be beans, salad, or a steak dinner. Sims take the unprepared ingredients from the fridge and search for a prep surface or food processor.

- If no prep surface is available, the meal morphs into a sorry can of cold beans, which the Sim eats immediately while standing. This is worth 16 Hunger points plus the points added by the refrigerator model—no better than a Quick Meal, actually.

- If a prep surface is available, the Sim uses it to chop up the ingredients. Then the Sim picks up the prepared food and searches for a cooking appliance. If none is found, the meal becomes a plate of salad. This is worth 16 Hunger points, plus the points added by the refrigerator model and the prep surface. Salad can be eaten sitting or standing.

Fig. 3-9. You need a countertop surface or a food processor to chop up the ingredients for a Full Meal.

- If the Sim finds a cooking appliance, the prepared food morphs into a "cooking state" (pot for stoves, tray for toaster oven or microwave). The Sim cooks the food; once it's removed from the appliance, it becomes a single plate of food—a steak dinner. This meal is worth 16 Hunger points plus the points added by refrigerator model, prep surface, and cooking appliance (which includes Cooking skill points). A steak dinner may be eaten sitting or standing.

Serve Breakfast/Lunch/Dinner (Group Meal)

This is a full platter of food with six servings. Depending on prep and cooking, it can be beans, salad, or a steak dinner. To start a Group Meal, Sims take unprepared ingredients from the fridge and search for a prep surface or food processor.

- If no prep surface is available, the meal morphs into a platter of—*wow!*—cans of beans. Your friends will go wild. Each serving of this rare feast increases the eater's Hunger motive score by 16 points plus the points added by the refrigerator model.

- Then the Sim picks up the prepared food and searches for a cooking appliance. If none is found, the meal becomes a group platter of salad. Each serving is worth 16 Hunger points, plus the points added by the refrigerator model and the prep surface.

Fig. 3-10. Nothing's more pathetic than a guy serving guests a platter full of cans of beans. Get a counter and a cooking appliance, fool.

- If the Sim finds a cooking appliance, the prepared food morphs into a "cooking state" (pot for stoves, tray for toaster oven or microwave). The Sim cooks the food; when it's removed from the appliance, it becomes a group platter of food—six steak dinners! Each serving is worth 16 Hunger points plus the points added by refrigerator model, prep surface, and cooking appliance (which includes Cooking skill points).

Gift Food Items

Visitors bearing gifts may offer two kinds of multiple-serving treats—candy and fruitcake.

Candy Box: Offers 12 servings per box. Can be placed on floor but eaten only if set on a table-height serving surface. Each serving offers three Hunger points. Always eaten standing up.

Fruitcake: Offers six festive slices. If not eaten, may be used as doorstop. OK, maybe not, but it can be served from both table-height surfaces and floor. Each serving adds seven Hunger points. Never goes bad with flies. Really. Always eaten standing up. (Only way to swallow it, apparently.) Neat Sims wash hands afterward, as would any intelligent being. Sims with a high Cooking skill enjoy fruitcake more.

After-Meal Cleanup (or Not)

Sloppy Sims leave dirty plates, pizza boxes, snack bags and other trash lying around the kitchen. (They drop snack bags on the floor, where each creates a small pile of trash.) Neat Sims, on the other hand, wash the dishes (or load the dishwasher) and throw away trash. When throwing away trash, a Sim picks up the pile (it becomes a plastic trash bag) and seeks to dispose of it in the following order:

1. Indoor trash can or trash compactor. If full, then:
2. Existing trash pile. If full, then:
3. Outdoor trash can.

Flies and Roaches

Dirty dishes and platters, Quick Meal boxes, and pizza boxes spawn flies after eight hours. All uneaten food goes bad and spawns flies after eight hours, too. Candy goes bad after 24 hours. (Again, fruitcake never goes bad. We think it has a half-life of 1,300 years, but Maxis won't confirm this.) Unfortunately, you can't kill flies. The only way to rid your home of their annoying buzz is to wash the dirty dishes and/or discard the trash.

Fig. 3-11. Bob's kitchen is a mess. Dirty dishes and other garbage attracts flies after eight hours.

The *Livin' Large* expansion pack adds a disgusting new pest to the mix—*roaches*. At a random time each day, roaches may spawn from dirty objects such as trash, dishes, ashes, tubs, and unmade beds. These swarming bugs bring down the Room score. Unlike flies, however, roaches can be exterminated. For more info on the vermin, find "Roaches" in the "List of Object Interactions" in chapter 9, "Sim Objects."

Comfort

Comfort is a straightforward need. To be comfortable, Sims need good furniture for seating or sleeping. In general, the better the chair, sofa, or bed, the more Comfort satisfaction it provides. But note that a nice hot bath can provide excellent Comfort, too. In fact, a luxurious soak in the §3,200 Hydrothera bathtub boosts your Comfort considerably.

Sims may acquire Comfort in tandem with other needs. Tubs boost Comfort and Hygiene at the same time. Beds boost Comfort and Energy at the same time. And, in some cases, you can build skills while boosting Comfort levels. (See the corresponding Tip.)

Note that the *Livin' Large* expansion pack adds some interesting new Comfort-related items. The Antique Lamp spouts a genie when you "Clean" it; the genie's Fire spell has a "good" outcome that sets the Sim user's Comfort

Fig. 3-12. What could be more comforting than reading a book on a balcony overlooking a pool while sitting in the maxi-comfort Von Braun recliner? Answer: Very little.

and Social motives to a full 100. (The "bad" outcome sets a flammable object on fire.)

Two other *Livin' Large* objects can dramatically *decrease* Comfort, as well. Using the Little Voodoo Dolly on another Sim causes that Sim's Comfort rating to bottom out at –100. (The affected Sim also seeks out and slaps the perpetrator.) And anyone who drinks the chartreuse-colored potion made with the Concatenation Station Home Chemistry Lab is in for an unhappy attack of "motive subtraction"—all of the drinker's motives are set to –70. Lucky for your Sims, drinking the blue-colored potion will counteract this and max out all of their motives.

For more detail on how these new *Livin' Large* objects work, look them up in the alphabetized "List of Object Interactions" in chapter 9, "Sim Objects."

Hygiene and Bladder

As a strategy guide, we feel badly when we can find little to say about certain aspects of a game. But really, what could be less tricky than Hygiene and Bladder needs? These two motives are so uncomplicated that we combined them into one section.

To raise Hygiene scores, engage your Sims in activities that clean them. Sneaky, eh? Take showers or baths to max out Hygiene. For quick boosts, go to the sink and wash hands, or use the medicine cabinet to brush teeth. You also gain a decent Hygiene boost from soaking in the hot tub.

To relieve the Bladder motive, you have two simple choices: use the toilet or have an accident. Bladder accidents provide full relief, but

Fig. 3-13. Oops. This guy should have gotten up sooner. Maybe he would have made it to the bathroom.

they leave an unsightly puddle and (as you might expect) push the soiled Sim's Hygiene score to the red end of the scale.

Fun

Fun is a personal, individual thing. Your idea of fun might be different from mine. And gee, isn't that what makes the world go 'round? This diversity is recognized in *The Sims*. As we discussed at length in chapter 2, "Personality," each Sim's personality structure (particularly the Playful trait) determines the activities a Sim will find most fun.

A simple example: Playful Sims are attracted to computer games, pinball, and doll-houses. Serious Sims—that is, Sims with a low Playful rating—tend to seek activities such as chess, reading, and viewing art objects. To fully understand how activities "broad-cast" fun to Sims, check out "Advertising" in chapter 4, "Sim "Autonomy.""

Max Fun

Most Fun-raising objects have a maximum fun (Max Fun) level—that is, a limit to how high that activity can raise the Fun motive score. If a Sim's Fun score is at 75, and the stereo's Max Fun is 80, the Sim will only dance until hitting 80 Fun points. After that, the Sim must interact with another object that has a Max Fun score higher than 80 to get any more Fun.

Again, personality can affect Max Fun by raising or lowering it for a particular object/activity.

TV, Music, and Fun

TV channels offer differing amounts of fun, depending on Sim personality. Here's a quick look at the TV fare certain Sim types prefer.

TYPE OF SIM	PREFERRED TV CHANNEL
Playful	Cartoon
Grouchy (Low Nice)	Horror
Active	Action
Outgoing	Romance

Although TV channels affect the amount of fun Sims get from TV watching, the same isn't true of their choice of genre in music. A Sim has no preference for music types—country over classical, for example, or rock over latin.

Kids and Fun

Fun matters more to kids, in general. Compared to adults, fun plays a bigger part in determining their mood, and it drains quickly, so kids have to do fun stuff a lot.

Energy

Energy is the third physical motive (along with Hunger and Bladder) you can't ignore if it drops very low. If an Energy score bottoms out at –100, the Sim will keel over backward and fall dead asleep on the floor . . . or sleep standing up, if there's no floor space. It's kind of amusing the first time it happens. After that, it's just sad.

The main way to replenish your Energy need is to sleep or nap, although coffee or espresso will give you a small shot of Energy. Sleep on any bed, or nap on any sofa or recliner chair.

Tips from the Testers

A profoundly limiting factor is the time constraint sleep puts on your busy Sims—too much to do, not enough Energy to do it. The less time your Sims spend sleeping, the better. One solution: get the most expensive bed as soon as possible. The Modern Mission bed boosts your Energy score faster during sleep. Thus, you can rise earlier and get more things done before going to work.

> Modern Mission Bed $3,000
> Patterned on the Arts and Crafts movement's design principles of simplicity and workmanship, our craftspeople have reinterpreted this aesthetic for the new millennium. Cherrywood and mahogany combine to create a luxurious place to sleep and re-energize.
> Comfort: 9
> Energy: 10
> Room: 3

Fig. 3-14. The Modern Mission Bed is a miracle of modern design, offering the best Energy boost known to Simdom—a perfect 10.

—Andrew Blomquist, Tester

Sleep

Sims spin happily into PJs before they go to sleep in bed. Generally, Sims sleep until "fully rested"—that is, until their Energy score hits a full 100. At night, however, Sims sleep until at least 6 a.m., regardless of whether or not they're fully rested. There is one way around this: if you queue something up behind sleep, when the Energy score reaches a full 100 points in the middle of the night, a Sim will get up, even if it's before 6 a.m.

> **NOTE**
> Sims actually have a hidden "relationship score" with the beds you place in their house. Every time a Sim sleeps in a bed, his or her attraction to that bed increases, making it more likely he or she will seek out that bed autonomously the next time they sleep. Thus, you can actually "train" your Sims to sleep in a specific bed.

Waking Up

In general, waking from sleep is long and slow for Lazy Sims, quicker for Active Sims. Sims rise in a cranky mood if you awaken them before they're fully rested (before their Energy score hits a full 100). Sims don't like being awakened by something noisy, either. Alarms going off in the room—clock, fire, or burglar—wake up both adults and kids. So does a fire.

Other events also wake adults, but not kids, if they occur in the same room: baby crying; TV or stereo/radio on; phone ringing; Sim death; Sim playing piano, pinball, or computer game; Sim on exercise machine. Oh, and one other sound awakens adult Sims—a ghostly howl. (See "Ghosts!" in chapter 5, "Social Interactions.")

Using the Alarm Clock

If you have an alarm clock in the room, you may select Set Alarm. When you set an alarm clock, it rings two hours before the car-pool arrival time of any sleeping Sim in the room. However, note that the alarm awakens *everyone* in the room, regardless of car-pool time or whether they're asleep on floor, couch, or bed. (It doesn't matter who set the alarm.) Also, the alarm will go off once for each employed Sim sleeping in the room, even if they have different car-pool times.

Once set, an alarm clock remains set until you direct a Sim to Unset Alarm.

Social

The Social motive is a powerful one in *The Sims*. And why not? As Will Wright comments in the foreword, "There seems to be some evidence that our intelligence is the result of a vicious feedback cycle, a cycle that begins with social behavior. . . . Most of the other high intelligence animals on Earth also seem to be highly social creatures (i.e. dolphins, chimpanzees)."

Because the social aspect of *The Sims* is integral to the game experience, we devoted an entire chapter to social interactions. For now, we simply point out that most interactions with other Sims affect your Sim's Social motive score. For an in-depth look at interactions that affect the Social motive, see chapter 5, "Social Interactions."

> **TIP**
>
> Sims don't need neighbors to keep their Social motive high. Just one family member can provide all of the needed social interactions. But without friends from outside the family, Sims can't climb very high in any career track.

Room

The Room motive is probably the least pressing motive in *The Sims*. In the weighted average that determines Mood, Room carries far less overall weight (especially at the low end) than do other motives. But a critically low Room score still can pull a Mood level down a bar or two. A Mood hovering around zero can make a lot of difference in job promotion, skill-building, friend-making, and other social activities.

Anyway, you love your Sims, right? You created them. You want them to be as happy as possible. So let's look at how Room score works. In general, the following factors influence your Sim's like or dislike for a room.

Fig. 3-15. Paintings hung on interior walls can increase a Room score.

Room Size: The bigger, the better.

Light Levels: Windows, doors, ambient light (day or night), and lamps impact light levels. The brighter, the better.

Number of Corners: The more, the better. (See the "Building" section.)

Positive and Negative Objects: Refer to the following topic for more on this.

Maintenance is important! Some household items need your care. A wilting violet or murky water in the fish tank are not uncommon. If you want a good Room score, don't forget to do routine maintenance: clean the tank, water the plants.

Tips from the Testers

If you need a quick Room score boost, light a fire in the fireplace. Any lit fireplace can make a huge difference in room score. They work especially well when placed outside and lit just before Sims go to work. Because the outside area counts as one big room, the lighted fireplace may significantly raise your Room score for Sims on their way to work.

—Andrew Blomquist, Tester

Fig. 3-16. A cheery, crackling fire in the fireplace greatly enhances Room score.

Positive/Negative Objects

Many objects have a positive effect on Room scores. The Buy mode catalog gives you a good idea of which these are. Below we've reproduced a super-secret Room Score table we smuggled out of Maxis. (Don't tell them you saw it here, OK?) This table lists many objects in the game that affect Room score, positively or negatively. It also lists the point increase or decrease each object causes.

Ha! Try finding something like that in an unauthorized strategy guide. Before we hit the table, though, here's a quick summary of objects with a negative impact on Inside Room Score.

- Trash
- Floods
- Dirty plates
- Meals with flies
- Full trash cans/compactors
- Dead plants
- Puddle or ash pile
- Dead fish in aquariums
- Dirty objects (shower, toilet, tub)
- Roaches

Tips from the Testers

Room score can have a big impact on how relationships go. Lights help this a lot. The §350 "Torchosteronne" floor lamp is one of the most cost-efficient items you can place to raise Room scores. Also, build very large rooms if you plan to use them for social activities or gaining skills. Rounding off corners with a few diagonal walls also helps boost scores.

—Jason Morales, Tester

Certain broken objects (computer, TV, pinball) directly lower Room score, too, but others (dishwasher, shower, sink) rely on leaky flooding for negative impact.

> **NOTE**
> Art objects add to Room Score based on their price, which randomly appreciates or depreciates daily.

Outside Room score is a different matter as it has its own algorithm. Time of day influences Outside Room score since the amount of light affects the score (more sunlight, higher score). As for objects, those that would negatively impact the Inside Room score also negatively impact an Outside Room score. All other objects count positively, once per number of tiles they occupy.

> **NOTE**
> The following Room score table includes new objects from the Livin' Large expansion pack.

HOW OBJECTS AFFECT ROOM SCORE

OBJECT	STATE/TYPE	ROOM SCORE CHANGE
Aquarium	Fish Alive	25
	Dirty	−25
	Dirty and/or Dead	−50
Ash	—	−10
Bar	Bachman	20
	Beach Boss	8
Bed	Unmade (Any Bed)	−10
	Made, Mission	30
	Made, Four-Poster	32
	Made (All others)	10

HOW OBJECTS AFFECT ROOM SCORE (continued)

OBJECT	STATE/TYPE	ROOM SCORE CHANGE
Bench	Gothic Revival	40
Chair	Manchester	32
	Parisienne	25
	Duke of Earle	16
	Empress	10
Christmas Tree	Alive	32
	Dead	−50
Clock: Grandfather	—	50
Computer	Broken	−25
Counter	Barcelona	15
Desk	Redmond	15
	O'Mann	16
Dresser	Fantzi	32
	Antique Armoire	20
	Oak Armoire	10
Estate Sale Piece	—	32
Fire	—	−100
Fireplace	Library Edition (Off)	20
	Library Edition (On)	75
	Worcestershire (Off)	15
	Worcestershire (On)	60
	Bostonian (Off)	10
	Bostonian (On)	45
	Modesto (Off)	5
	Modesto (On)	30
Flamingo	—	10
Flood	—	−25
Flowers (Outdoor)	Healthy	20
	Dead	−20
Flowers/Plants (Indoor)	Dead	−10
	Healthy	10
	Wilted	0
Food	Snack (Spoiled)	−15
	Fruitcake (Empty Plate)	−5
	BBQ Group Meal (Spoiled)	−20
	BBQ Single Meal (Spoiled)	−15
	Empty Plate	−10

OBJECT	STATE/TYPE	ROOM SCORE CHANGE
	Pizza Slice (Spoiled)	−10
	Pizza Box (Spoiled)	−25
	Candy (Spoiled)	−5
	Group Meal (Spoiled)	−20
	Meal (Spoiled)	−25
	Quick Meal (Spoiled)	−20
Fountain	—	25
Gift Flowers	Dead	−10
	Alive	20
Head-in-jar Curio	—	32
Lamp	Not Broken	10
	Antique	8
Love 'n Haight Lamp	—	20
Mirror	Baroque Optilopticon	16
Newspaper	Old Newspapers	−20
Piano	—	30
Pinball Machine	Broken	−15
Rug	Leopard	16
	Schwa	32
	Persian, Bearskin, Tiger	54
Shower	Broken	−15
Sofa/Loveseat	Deiter or Dolce	20
	Red Matter	24
	Le Grande Guignol	32
Stereo	Strings	25
Suit of Armor	—	100
Table	Mesa	15
	M Table	16
	El Tomayo	24
	Parisienne	25
Toilet	Clogged	−10
Train Set: Small	—	25
Trash Can: Inside	Full	−20
Trash Compactor	Full	−25
Trash Pile	—	−20
TV	Soma	20
	Broken (Any TV)	−15

Motive Failure States

If you ignore or intentionally obstruct your Sims' physical needs, bad (and embarrassing) things happen. Of the eight motives, only Hunger, Energy, and Bladder can "fail."

At low levels, Hunger decays very slowly, and it motivates autonomous Sims to eat. So Hunger fails rarely unless you intentionally create a failure situation. The Energy and Bladder motives decrease at a fixed rate, however, and can be further stimulated by particularly draining (or filling) activities.

When Energy fails, your Sim falls asleep on the spot. When Bladder fails, well, take a wild guess. When Hunger fails—see the following topic, "Death."

Death

Ah, yes. The Big Sleep. When you goof up and lose a Sim to one of the the following mistakes, you get this curious message: "Though the body is gone, the spirit will always remain." Now what do you suppose that means? (Hint: For more on this, see "Ghosts" at the end of chapter 5, "Social Interactions.")

Fig. 3-17. Rest in peace, Quo. You were a good little guy. Will we ever see Quo again? Read the message carefully.

Tips from the Testers

Need to get rid of an extra Sim or two? Build a small swimming pool (3-by-3) with a ladder. Direct the extra Sims into the pool, and then remove the ladder. When the Sims run out of Energy, they drown. As an added bonus, you may sell the resulting tombstones for §5 each.

—Syruss Flyte, Tester

NOTE
Think of extra Sims as those expendable Star Trek guys in Federation uniforms who beam down to the planet surface to be killed by the threat Kirk and Spock vanquish in the end. We just hope Syruss never gets his hands on weapons of mass destruction.

Electrocution

Sims without Mechanical skill should keep their distance from a broken TV. Call a Repairman, instead. With 0 Mechanical points, a Sim stands a 100 percent chance of getting electrocuted if the Sim tries to repair a TV. With 1 skill point, the odds of death drop to 25 percent. With 2 points, the chance is only 10 percent. At every skill level (3 to 10) above that, the chance of electrocution is 1 percent.

Lamps can electrocute, too, if Sims change burned-out light bulbs. (Outdoor garden lamps require no light bulb changes.) But the odds are small—only 1 in 100 for every Sim, regardless of Mechanical skill level. After any electrocution, an urn stands where the Sim once stood. Repairmen never get electrocuted.

> **NOTE**
> Visitors can die by fire, as well.

Fire Death

When Sims die by fire, they flail around and then, in the words of the design spec document, "do a one-tile Wicked Witch 'I'm melting' kind of crumple." (Flames around a burning Sim obstruct most of this animation from view.) A burial urn appears immediately at the end of the gruesome spectacle. Once a Sim is set ablaze, however, another Sim can save him or her with a fire extinguisher. But you'd better be quick about it.

Fig. 3-18. Sims can live for days with low Hunger and give you plenty of warning that starvation lies ahead. For example, this woman needs a burger, BAD.

Starvation

A Sim's Hunger rating decays very, very slowly at low levels. So it takes Sims a *lo-o-o-o-ong* time to starve to death. Days, in fact. What a pleasant thought! But the point is, Sims don't drop dead suddenly of hunger with little warning. They let you know when they're hungry by waving, yelling, and displaying the "I Need Food!" icon over their heads. And they seek food autonomously (if you have Free Will checked in the Options box) unless you keep them busy with your Big God Orders, you power-hound.

However, Sims *will* starve if they have no means of obtaining food—no fridge and no money for pizza, or they're trapped somehow by, say, sadistic architecture. When this happens, the poor Sim falls to the floor in the fetal position and turns into a burial urn.

LIVIN' LARGE with The Grim Reaper

The *Livin' Large* expansion pack adds a new twist to death in *The Sims*: gamblin' with the Grim Reaper! Whenever a Sim dies, the infamous cloaked entity slowly floats to the corpse, waves his scythe, and conducts a ghostly ceremony to usher the poor unfortunate's soul into the beyond.

But guess what? You can talk to the guy! In fact, any adult Sim active on the lot can plead with the Grim Reaper for the life of the deceased Sim. But hurry—click on the hooded fellow and select "Plea" before he finishes his ceremony. If the Reaper deigns to consider a mortal entreaty, he engages the Sim supplicant in a game of "Rock, Paper, Scissors."

If the Reaper wins, one of two things can happen. Either he takes the soul, but leaves behind a greenish zombie with a blank personality instead of the robust Sim you once knew, or your Sim just flat out dies. If your Sim wins, the Reaper conducts another ceremony bringing the ex-Sim fully back to life.

4
Sim Autonomy

As Neighborhood God, your job (unless you choose some capricious Chaldean deity as your role model) is to keep your Sims happy—that is, in a good mood. One way to do this is to micromanage their lives, directing them moment by moment to engage in interactions that fulfill their needs—kind of like most guys' moms.

But a better God is One who truly understands His or Her Sims and their motivations. A Good God creates friendly, efficient environments so Sims can find a measure of happiness on their own, too. We take a closer look here at what Will Wright calls the game's "Happyscape"—the complex internal logic that drives Sims to seek, on their own, the most "happy-making" interaction available.

A Note About the Queue

As *The Sims* manual explains, you can queue as many as eight interactions for each Sim in your household. When left to act autonomously, however, Sims queue only one interaction at a time. They have very small brains, you see. Your Sim performs a chosen interaction, waits a few seconds, and then picks another interaction. However, your orders always take precedence. Selecting an interaction for your Sims cancels from the queue any action they may have chosen for themselves.

> **NOTE**
> To cancel any interaction, whether chosen by you or your Sim, click on its icon in the queue. A red X appears over the icon. When the Sim exits the interaction, the icon disappears. (Be patient. Sometimes your Sim needs a few seconds to terminate cancelled interactions fully.)

How Sims Make "Free Will" Decisions

In lieu of orders from God (you), Sims with Free Will do their own thing. On the surface, their choices seem straightforward, based on needs. "I'm hungry, so I will eat. My energy is low, so I will sleep." And, in general, that's exactly how it works.

But it's not as simple as just picking the lowest motive score and choosing an activity that increases it. A variety of factors can influence a Sim's calculation of needs. Moreover, in *The Sims*, objects actually drive the decision-making process by "advertising" their wondrous benefits to your little people. Some advertise falsely. What exactly does that mean? Read on.

Fig. 4-1. With the Free Will box marked, your Sims live life on THEIR terms unless you step in with your own directives.

Advertising

In essence, each possible interaction in the household—whether with a couch, a food processor, a lawn flamingo, or another Sim—calls like a carnival barker. "Hey, brush your teeth for Hygiene 25 here!" shouts the bathroom medicine cabinet. "Yo, I got 30 Comfort for a good sit, my man," says the living room's green plaid sofa.

Your autonomous Sim sorts through these tempting offers and selects the four activities that will make him or her happiest. Then, unless one candidate muscles its way to the front of the queue (see the following "Priority Interactions" section), your Sim selects randomly from among them.

Will Wright calls this incessant harangue "advertising." Each potential interaction broadcasts an "ad" touting how happy it can make your Sim by raising a certain motive score.

> **NOTE**
>
> Sim neighbors are "smarter" than the Sims you control in the active household. Visitors always choose the best activity available to raise their mood, unlike your current Sims, who choose randomly from among the top four.

Priority Interactions

Household Sims don't always choose wisely on their own. Because they select randomly from the four highest advertised candidates, one of every four choices will rank lowest.

Priority interactions, however, *always* get picked if they're the highest rated of the four. These include Sleep (highly advertised when the Energy score is low), Use Toilet (highly advertised when Bladder is low), or one of the eat-food commands (Make Dinner, Have Snack, and the like) when Hunger is low.

Fig. 4-2. Using the toilet is a priority interaction for autonomous Sims. That is, Sims select it automatically if it's the highest advertised interaction.

Fig. 4-3. When a fire breaks out, Sims come running in a Panic reaction that pushes its way to the front of the queue, regardless of their other needs.

"Push" Interactions

Certain other interactions bypass this sorting process, however. These special choices "push" to the front of the queue, ignoring the top four. These interactions include Wash Hands after eating pizza or using the toilet (for Sims with a high Neat trait); Panic, if a fire breaks out; Go to Work (if the Sim is in a good mood, of course); and Move Out of the Way (the icon with the two footprints), if your Sim blocks another Sim's path. Note that you can delete these interactions by deleting them from your Sims queue.

False Advertising

Some interactions advertise falsely. They lure the autonomous Sim by promising fulfillment of a real need, but they don't actually raise that motive score. A good example is the phone. When it rings, the interaction "Answer" advertises 50 points each of Fun, Comfort, and Social fulfillment. But the act of answering the phone fulfills none of these needs— not directly, anyway.

Another example is the somber interaction Mourn. In the first 24 hours after a death, a deceased Sim's tombstone or urn advertises a whopping 50 points of Comfort, Fun, Hygiene, Social, and Room! Therefore, your household Sims are *very* motivated to mourn their dearly departed that first day.

Fig. 4-4. The Mourn interaction advertises powerfully for 24 hours after a Sim death. It lures with false advertising, however, offering a 50-point increase for each of 5 needs, but satisfying none.

Ad Modifiers

Three factors influence an ad's attractiveness—the Sim's personality, current motive scores, and distance from the beckoning object.

How Personality Modifies Choice

In chapter 2, "Personality," we discussed personality influences on Sim behavior in general terms. What follows is a more specific examination of how this works.

When a personality trait "modifies" an activity, it actually raises or lowers the point value of the ad that activity broadcasts. The more points of the personality trait the Sim has, the more points that trait contributes to the activity's ad.

Say, for example, a Sim with low Fun points stands in his living room. The big-screen Soma Plasma TV and the Down Wit' Dat boom box sit in the same room. The TV interaction Turn On broadcasts an ad of 49 Fun, and the boom box interaction Dance broadcasts an ad of 50 Fun. Which does your Sim choose?

> **NOTE**
> For a complete list of possible object interactions, their ads, and the personality traits that modify the ads, see the "Object Advertising" table later in this chapter.

Fig. 4-5. Two activities—Turn On (the TV) and Dance (at the boom box)—advertise the same amount of Fun points. Because her Active trait is high, Betty chooses to dance; Bob chooses TV because he's, well, lazy.

Other things being equal, the Sim will choose to dance. But other things are rarely equal in *The Sims*. In this case, the choice depends on how many Active points you've assigned to this Sim's personality index. The Active/Lazy scale modifies the amount of Fun points both activities advertise, but in opposite ways. For a Lazy (low Active) Sim, the TV will advertise a high number of points, while an Active Sim's personality will take away points from the TV, so it advertises less. The Active Sim, however, will get more points from the Dance ad. Even if your Sim is just a little on the Lazy side, he'll gravitate to the tube. Of course, an Active Sim looking for Fun points will boogie at the boom box. In the Object Advertising Table later in this section, the values you see are the highest they can be. Depending on personality, the ad values may drop for a certain object.

How Motive Scores Modify Ad Choice

Again, household objects advertise an increase in motive scores for certain activities—35 Fun to play chess, 40 Room to wind the grandfather clock, and so on. Certain personality traits modify these ads a bit. After that, your autonomous Sim chooses activities that offer the greatest score increase, right? Wrong. As the motive score changes, the amount of happiness a Sim derives from raising that score changes, as well.

Whew! This may seem complicated, but it's a basic phenomenon that mirrors your own life decisions and the circumstances that affect them. (We explain in detail how Sims calculate happiness in the following section, "Happiness Contribution Curves.")

Here's a simple, common sense example. If a Sim is very low on both Hunger and Fun, then, which type of ad (Hunger-satisfying or Fun-satisfying) will most attract his or her attention? Obviously, the best Hunger ad will carry far more weight. As in real life, the more eating meals raises a Sim's Hunger score, the less appeal Hunger-fulfilling ads will have. After you eat a hearty steak dinner, those mouth-watering food ads on TV have far less allure.

Fig. 4-6. Your life is dull, and you're starving. Which need do you fulfill first? Answer: SNACK TIME! A critical need such as Hunger increases in importance as its score drops.

Happiness Contribution Curves

OK, if the section on calculating mood with weighted averages in chapter 3, "Mood and Motives" fascinated you, stay with us here. Otherwise, you probably know all you need (or care) to know about how motive scores affect Sim decision-making. Just skip to the "Ad Attenuation" section, because what follows here is for Sim-lovers who want to peel away yet another layer and poke fingers at the innards of Sim autonomy.

First, understand that the happiness an interaction offers your Sim differs from the motive point increase that interaction advertises. Why? Because a curve that calculates a "happiness contribution value" modifies the ad's point increase. Your Sim bases his or her autonomous decisions on this value.

The happiness contribution value is determined using the following steps.

1. Your Sim "hears" the ad for some interaction. The ad offers an increase in some motive score. Let's use two examples for the sake of comparison: a refrigerator advertising Hunger 70 to "Have Dinner" and a stereo advertising Fun 70 to "Dance."

2. In essence, your Sim asks, "How happy will a 70-point Hunger increase make me compared to a 70-point Fun increase?" (Of course, she's also comparing the happiness value of numerous other ads, but we'll stick to these two for simplicity's sake.)

3. To determine this, your Sim takes the advertised point increase for each motive (70 Hunger for "Have Dinner" and 70 Fun for "Dance") and converts each into "happiness contribution points." How?

4. First, she determines her current motive scores. For this example, let's say her Fun score is at –20 and her Hunger score has dropped to –70. (Yes, our gal's nearing death.)

5. Now she uses a "happiness contribution curve" (different for each motive) to calculate the happiness contribution of each advertised interaction. These curves (seen below) modify ads depending on the current score of the motive being advertised.

6. Take a look at the following charts. Don't worry, they're straightforward and probably won't hurt you. Note that the graph's horizontal "x-axis" values represent the range of current motive scores (from –100 to 100). The graph's vertical "y-axis" values represent the range of happiness contribution value.

7. Let's calculate the happiness value increase for the "Have Dinner" ad first. On the Hunger graph, find the current motive value on the x-axis—in this case, –70. Then move straight up and mark the point where –70 intersects the Hunger curve. Label it Point A, as we did on our graph above.

8. Now calculate how much your Hunger score will increase if you "Have Dinner." Simple math: Starting at –70 (current Hunger score) on the x-axis, move 70 points to the right along the axis. You end up at 0. This will be your final Hunger score if you eat dinner.

9. Now go straight up and mark where 0 intersects the Hunger curve. Call it Point B.

10. Follow the curve from Point A to Point B. How much is the vertical (y-axis) rise? In this case, you go up from –44 to 43, a total rise of 87 points. This increase is the "happiness contribution value."

11. Follow the same process to plot the happiness contribution value for a "Dance" at the stereo, figuring the "happiness value" rise from the Fun motive's starting score of –20 going up 70 points to 50. In this case, a Fun motive point rise of 70 yields a "happiness value" increase of only 40 points.

12. Thus, even though a stereo dance advertises the same rise in absolute motive points (70), dinner actually increases your very hungry Sim's overall happiness far, far more (87 to 40) in this particular case.

You can see how the happiness contribution curves get steeper in the very low ranges for each motive. This means that when motives get very low, even a small increase in motive points can produce a large happiness contribution value. As in real life, this is particularly true for physical needs such as Hunger, Bladder, and Comfort.

Ad Attenuation

Most ads "attenuate" over distance. That is, the beckoning interactions grow weaker and eventually dissipate to silence as your Sim moves away from them. Certain ads attenuate less than others, though. For example, a bed's attractiveness remains the same whether a Sim is near or far. On the other hand, most Fun-satisfying objects advertise only to nearby Sims, usually those in the same room.

The Sims measures this attenuation in three increments: ads with high attenuation have a short broadcast range and attract the attention of nearby Sims; ads with medium attenuation broadcast a little farther; Sims can "hear" ads with low attenuation almost anywhere on the lot.

Fig. 4-7. While she stands near her mailbox, this Sim can't "hear" ads for Fun broadcasting from the living room TV or stereo because they attenuate (sort of stretch out and fade) quickly over distance.

Most low-attenuation ads are broadcast by activities that fulfill urgent needs—Hunger, Energy, and Bladder. The WhirlWizard hot tub and Aristoscratch pool table are notable exceptions, broadcasting far and wide their ads to Join.

> **NOTE**
> For a complete list of household interactions and their levels of attenuation, see the "Object Advertising" table later in this chapter.

Exit Conditions

A Sim will exit prolonged interactions automatically under certain conditions. Hey, you can only play computer games for so long (unless you're an unmarried programmer). These "exit conditions" allow autonomous Sims to live some semblance of a normal life and not act like little obsessive-compulsive types. Exit conditions also allow you to queue interactions and have your Sim spend some time in each interaction.

> **NOTE**
> To exit an interaction before it meets exit conditions, click on its icon to delete it from the queue.

When certain motives drop below a critical value, a Sim will exit an interaction. A balloon that pops up over the Sim's head displays an icon to represent the critically low motive. The value differs for household members and visitors.

MOTIVE (SIM TYPE)	SIM EXITS CURRENT INTERACTION WHEN MOTIVE DROPS BELOW
Hunger (Resident)	−80
Hunger (Visitor)	−40
Bladder (Resident)	−85
Bladder (Visitor)	−80
Energy (Resident)	−80
Energy (Visitor)	−70
Comfort (Resident)	−90
Comfort (Visitor)	−60

Fig. 4-8. Sims wave and let you know (using thought balloons) which needs are particularly low. This gal could use a dose of Comfort.

Additional exit conditions differ slightly for Fun objects, Skill objects, and Repair objects (listed in the following paragraphs.)

Exiting Repair Activities

When a mood score drops below –50 (between two and three red bars on the Mood Indicator), that Sim is too bummed out to continue Repair work on the computer, dishwasher, espresso machine, hot tub, lamp, pinball, shower, sink, toilet, or TV.

Exiting Skill-Building Activities

If a mood score drops below 0 (red bars on the Mood Indicator), that Sim is too depressed to continue honing skills using a bookshelf, chessboard, exercise machine, easel, piano, mirror, medicine cabinet, woodworking table, telescope, or guitar. Also, chess games have a set length: Sims will exit chess when the game ends. (You can just start another game.) And Sims will stop painting at the easel when they finish each work. (To continue, just sell the work and start painting again.)

> **NOTE**
> Sims exit any Skill-building activity automatically when they earn a Skill point or if another inter-action is in their queue.

Fig. 4-9. Bob needs Logic points to advance in his chosen career, but he's too depressed to play chess. Get his motive scores out of the red to cheer him up. Then try again.

Exiting Fun Activities

In the following Fun activities, Sims will exit the interaction once the Fun score raises to the object's maximum points. (Remember, this Max Fun score varies according to a Sim's personality type.)

- Basketball Hoop
- Beverage Bar
- Bookshelf (Read Book)
- Christmas Tree
- Computer (Play)
- Dollhouse
- Fireworks Kit
- Guinea Pig
- Guitar
- Jukebox
- Piano
- Pinball Machine
- Play Structure
- Slot Machine
- Stereo
- Telescope
- Toy Box
- Train Set
- TV
- Voodoo Dolly
- VR Headset

The following Fun-satisfying interactions offer one-shot interactions that have no exit or refuse conditions. To raise a Fun score to its maximum, a Sim may have to repeat the activity several times.

- Aquarium (Feed or Watch Fish)
- Baby (Play)
- Espresso Machine (Drink)
- Diving Board (Dive In)
- Fountain (View)
- Love 'n Haight Lamp (View)
- Painting (View)
- Sculpture (View)

The following Fun-satisfying objects have a preset game length. Again, for maximum Fun points, a Sim may have to repeat the activity.

- Chessboard
- Pool Table

Sims won't exit a hot tub until all the motives it raises (Fun, Comfort, Social, Hygiene) reach their maximum. The pool has no exit conditions; Sims continue swimming until another motive ad calls them out, or you give them another direction.

Fig. 4-10. Once Sims hop in the hot tub, they tend to hang awhile. In fact, they won't leave autonomously until all four motives satisfied by the experience hit their max.

Object Advertising Table

The following game objects advertise their ability to satisfy Sim needs. The table lists objects alphabetically, and shows the interactions possible with each object, which motive and how many points each interaction advertises, which (if any) personality trait increases the object's ad value, and the level of attenuation for each ad's broadcast.

Object Type	Possible Interactions	Object Variations	Motive Advertised	Ad Value	Personality Trait Modifier	Ad Attenuation
Antique Lamp						
	View					
		Antique Lamp	Fun	5		High
Aquarium						
	Clean & restock					
		Aquarium	Room	30	Neat	Medium
	Feed Fish					
		Aquarium	Room	10	Nice	High
		Aquarium	Fun	10	Playful	High
	Watch Fish					
		Aquarium	Fun	10	Playful	High
Ash						
	Sweep Up					
		Ash	Energy	23		Medium
		Ash	Room	50	Neat	Medium

Object Type	Possible Interactions	Object Variations	Motive Advertised	Ad Value	Personality Trait Modifier	Ad Attenuation
Baby						
	Play					
		Baby	Fun	50	Playful	Medium
Bar						
	Have a drink					
		Any Bar	Room	30		Low
Barbecue						
	Grill					
		Barbecue	Energy	−10		Low
		Barbecue	Hunger	40	Cooking	Low
Basketball Hoop						
	Join					
		Basketball Hoop	Fun	30	Active	High
		Basketball Hoop	Social	20		Medium
		Basketball Hoop	Energy	−20		Medium
	Play					
		Basketball Hoop	Fun	30	Active	High
		Basketball Hoop	Energy	−20		High
Bed						
	Make Bed					
		All Beds	Room	25	Neat	High
	Sleep					
		Bed double (Cheap Eaze)	Energy	65		None
		Bed double (Napoleon)	Energy	67		None
		Bed double (Mission)	Energy	70		None
		Bed double (Four-Poster)	Energy	70		None
		Bed double (Vibromatic)	Energy	70		None
		Bed single (Spartan)	Energy	60		None
		Bed single (Tyke Nyte)	Energy	63		None
	Tuck in Kid					
		All Beds	Energy	160	Nice	None
	Play in Bed					
		Vibromatic	Social	80		Low
		Vibromatic	Fun	80		Low

Object Type	Possible Interactions	Object Variations	Motive Advertised	Ad Value	Personality Trait Modifier	Ad Attenuation
Bookshelf						
	Read a Book					
		Bookshelf (Pine)	Fun	10	Serious	High
		Bookshelf (Amishim)	Fun	20	Serious	High
		Bookshelf (Libri di Regina, Swing)	Fun	30	Serious	High
Chair: Living Room						
	Sit					
		Wicker	Comfort	20		Medium
		Country Class	Comfort	20		Medium
		Citronel	Comfort	20		Medium
		Sarrbach	Comfort	20		Medium
		Duke of Earle	Comfort	20		Medium
		Ebonized Victorian	Comfort	20		Medium
		Manchester	Comfort	20		Medium
		Egg	Comfort	20		Medium
		Etherette	Comfort	20		Medium
		Frogg	Comfort	20		Medium
		Satanistics	Comfort	20		Medium
Chair: Dining						
	Sit					
		Werkbunnst	Comfort	25		Medium
		Teak	Comfort	25		Medium
		Empress	Comfort	25		Medium
		Parisienne	Comfort	25		Medium
		The "M"	Comfort	25		Medium
		El Tomayo	Comfort	25		Medium
		Sir Laxalot	Comfort	25		Medium
Chair: Office/Deck						
	Sit					
		Office Chair	Comfort	20		Medium
		Deck Chair	Comfort	20		Medium
Chair: Recliner						
	Nap					
		Both Recliners	Energy	15	Lazy	High
		Both Recliners	Comfort	20	Lazy	Medium
	Sit					
		Both Recliners	Comfort	30	Lazy	Medium

Object Type	Possible Interactions	Object Variations	Motive Advertised	Ad Value	Personality Trait Modifier	Ad Attenuation
Chemistry Set						
	Drink Potion					
		Chemistry Set	Hunger	40		Low
		Chemistry Set	Fun	0		Low
Chess						
	Join					
		Chess Set	Fun	40	Outgoing	High
		Chess Set	Social	40		Medium
	Play					
		Chess Set	Fun	35	Serious	High
Clock: Cuckoo						
	View					
		Cuckoo Clock	Fun	15		High
Clock: Grandfather						
	Wind					
		Grandfather Clock	Room	40	Neat	High
Coffee Espresso machine						
	Drink Espresso					
		Coffee Espresso machine	Energy	115		Medium
		Coffee Espresso machine	Fun	10		High
		Coffee Espresso machine	Bladder	−10		High
	Repair					
Coffeemaker						
	Drink Coffee					
		Coffeemaker	Bladder	−5		High
		Coffeemaker	Energy	115		Medium
Computer						
	Play					
		Computer (Moneywell)	Fun	30	Playful	High
		Computer (Microscotch)	Fun	35	Playful	High
		Computer (Brahma)	Fun	40	Playful	High
		Computer (Marco)	Fun	50	Playful	High
	Turn Off					
		All Computers	Energy	220	Neat	Medium

Object Type	Possible Interactions	Object Variations	Motive Advertised	Ad Value	Personality Trait Modifier	Ad Attenuation
Dollhouse						
	Play					
		Dollhouse	Fun	30	Playful	High
	Watch					
		Dollhouse	Fun	30	Playful	Medium
		Dollhouse	Social	30		Medium
Easel						
	Paint					
		Easel	Fun	20		High
Estate Sale Piece						
	View					
		Estate Sale Piece	Fun	5		High
Fireworks Kit						
	Light					
		Fireworks	Fun	30	Playful	Medium
	Watch Fireworks		Mood	100		High
	Watch Fireworks		Fun	100		High
Flamingo						
	Kick					
		Flamingo	Mood	15	Grouchy	High
	View					
		Flamingo	Fun	10	Playful	High
Flood						
	Clean					
		Flood	Room	80	Neat	High
Flowers (Outdoor)						
	Stomp On					
		All Flowers	Mood	10	Grouchy	High
	Water					
		All Flowers	Room	20	Neat	Medium
Flowers/Plants (Indoor)						
	Throw out					
		All Flowers/Plants	Room	50	Neat	Medium
	Water					
		All Flowers/Plants	Room	25	Neat	Medium

OBJECT TYPE	POSSIBLE INTERACTIONS	OBJECT VARIATIONS	MOTIVE ADVERTISED	AD VALUE	PERSONALITY TRAIT MODIFIER	AD ATTENUATION
Food						
	Clean					
		All Meal/ Snack types	Room	20	Neat	Medium
	Prepare and Eat					
		Food - BBQ Group Meal	Hunger	90		Low
		Food - BBQ Single	Hunger	80		Low
		Food - Candy	Hunger	30		Low
		Food - Fruit Cake Group Meal	Hunger	30		Low
		Food - Fruit Cake Slice	Hunger	80		Low
		Food - Light Meal	Hunger	80		Low
		Food - Pizza Box	Hunger	90		Low
		Food - Pizza Slice	Hunger	80		Low
		Food - Regular Group Meal	Hunger	90		Low
		Food - Regular Meal Single	Hunger	80		Low
		Food - Snack	Hunger	25		Low
Fountain						
	Play					
		Fountain	Fun	10	Shy	High
Fridge						
	Have [Meal]					
		All Fridges	Hunger	65		Low
	Have a Snack					
		Llamark	Hunger	20		Low
		Porcina	Hunger	30		Low
		Freeze Secret	Hunger	40		Low
		Old Thyme	Hunger	40		Low
	Have Quick [Meal]					
		All Fridges	Hunger	55		Low
	Serve [Meal]					
		All Fridges	Hunger	70	Cooking	Low
		All Fridges	Energy	−10		Low
Garden Gnome						
	Kick					
		Garden Gnome	Fun	60		High

Object Type	Possible Interactions	Object Variations	Motive Advertised	Ad Value	Personality Trait Modifier	Ad Attenuation
Garden Gnome, continued						
	Kick, continued					
		Garden Gnome	Comfort	60		High
		Garden Gnome	Social	60		High
Gift Flowers						
	Clean					
		Gift Flowers	Room	30	Neat	Medium
Guinea Pig						
	Play					
		Guinea Pig	Fun	10	Nice	High
	Clean					
		Guinea Pig	Room	30	Neat	High
	Feed					
		Guinea Pig	Room	10	Neat	High
		Guinea Pig	Fun	10	Nice	High
Guitar						
	Play					
		Guitar	Fun	40	Creativity	High
	Watch					
		Guitar	Social	100		Medium
		Guitar	Fun	70		Medium
Head in Jar						
	View					
		Head in Jar	Fun	5		High
Hot Tub						
	Get in					
		Hot Tub	Fun	45	Lazy	High
		Hot Tub	Comfort	50		High
		Hot Tub	Social	25	Outgoing	Medium
		Hot Tub	Hygiene	5		Medium
	Join					
		Hot Tub	Comfort	30		Low
		Hot Tub	Fun	50	Outgoing	Low
		Hot Tub	Social	50		Low
		Hot Tub	Hygiene	5		Medium
Love 'n Haight Lamp						
	Turn On					
		Love 'n Haight Lamp	Room	5		High
	View					
		Love 'n Haight Lamp	Fun	5		High

Object Type	Possible Interactions	Object Variations	Motive Advertised	Ad Value	Personality Trait Modifier	Ad Attenuation
Mailbox						
	Get Mail					
		Mailbox	Comfort	10		High
		Mailbox	Hunger	10		High
		Mailbox	Hygiene	10		High
		Mailbox	Room	10		High
Medicine Cabinet						
	Brush Teeth					
		Medicine Cabinet	Hygiene	25	Neat	Medium
Moose Head						
	View					
		Moose Head	Fun	8	Shy	High
Newspaper						
	Clean Up					
		Newspaper	Room	50	Neat	Medium
	Read					
		Newspaper	Fun	5	Serious	High
Painting/Wall Hanging						
	View					
		All Paintings/ Hangings	Fun	5	Serious	High
Phone						
	Answer					
		Both Phones	Fun	50		Medium
		Both Phones	Comfort	50		Medium
		Both Phones	Social	50		Medium
	Service/Pizza					
		Both Phones	Hunger	10		Low
Piano						
	Play					
		Both Pianos	Fun	40	Creativity	High
	Watch					
		Both Pianos	Fun	70		Medium
		Both Pianos	Social	10		Medium
Pinball Machine						
	Join					
		Pinball machine	Fun	50		Medium
		Pinball machine	Social	30		Medium
	Play					
		Pinball machine	Fun	40	Playful	High

Object Type	Possible Interactions	Object Variations	Motive Advertised	Ad Value	Personality Trait Modifier	Ad Attenuation
Play Structure						
	Join					
		Play Structure	Fun	60	Playful	Medium
		Play Structure	Social	40		Medium
	Play					
		Play Structure	Fun	60	Playful	Medium
Pool Diving Board						
	Dive In					
		Pool Diving Board	Fun	35	Active	High
		Pool Diving Board	Energy	−10		High
Pool Table						
	Join					
		Pool Table	Fun	50	Playful	Low
		Pool Table	Social	40		Low
	Play					
		Pool Table	Fun	45	Playful	High
Roaches						
	Freak Out					
		Roaches	Hygiene	100	Neat	Medium
		Roaches	Room	200	Neat	Medium
		Roaches	Mood	100	Neat	Medium
	Stomp					
		Roaches	Hygiene	40		Medium
		Roaches	Room	100		Medium
		Roaches	Mood	40		Medium
Sculpture						
	View					
		Scylla and Charybdis	Fun	6	Serious	High
		Large Black Slab	Fun	8	Serious	High
		China Vase	Fun	7	Serious	High
		All Other Sculptures	Fun	5	Serious	High
Shower						
	Clean					
		Shower	Room	20	Neat	High
	Take a Shower					
		Shower	Hygiene	50	Neat	Medium

Object Type	Possible Interactions	Object Variations	Motive Advertised	Ad Value	Personality Trait Modifier	Ad Attenuation
Sink						
	Wash Hands					
		All Sinks	Hygiene	10	Neat	High
Sofa/Loveseat						
	Nap					
		All Sofas/ Loveseats	Energy	40	Lazy	High
		All Sofas/ Loveseats	Comfort	5	Lazy	High
	Sit					
		All Sofas/ Loveseats	Comfort	30	Lazy	Medium
		Both Benches	Comfort	30	Lazy	Medium
Stereo						
	Dance					
		Boom Box	Social	40	Outgoing	High
		Boom Box	Fun	50	Active	High
		Zimantz Hi-Fi	Social	50	Outgoing	High
		Zimantz Hi-Fi	Fun	60	Active	High
		Strings Theory	Social	60	Outgoing	High
		Strings Theory	Fun	70	Active	High
		Wurl 'n Hurl	Social	60	Outgoing	High
		Wurl 'n Hurl	Fun	70	Active	High
	Join					
		Boom Box	Social	40	Outgoing	Low
		Boom Box	Fun	40	Outgoing	Low
		Zimantz Hi-Fi	Social	50	Outgoing	Low
		Zimantz Hi-Fi	Fun	40	Outgoing	Low
		Strings Theory	Social	60	Outgoing	Low
		Strings Theory	Fun	40	Outgoing	Low
		Wurl 'n Hurl	Social	60	Outgoing	Low
		Wurl 'n Hurl	Fun	40	Outgoing	Low
	Turn Off					
		All Stereos	Energy	220	Neat	Medium
	Turn On					
		Boom Box	Fun	25	Playful	High
		Zimantz Hi-Fi	Fun	25	Playful	High
		Strings Theory	Fun	30	Playful	High
		Wurl 'n Hurl	Fun	30	Playful	High

Object Type	Possible Interactions	Object Variations	Motive Advertised	Ad Value	Personality Trait Modifier	Ad Attenuation
Suit of Armor						
	View					
		Suit of Armor	Fun	5		High
Telescope						
	Gaze					
		Telescope	Fun	30	Serious	High
Toilet						
	Clean					
		All Toilets	Room	40	Neat	High
	Flush					
		Hygeia-O-Matic	Room	30	Neat	High
	Unclog					
		All Toilets	Room	50	Neat	High
	Use					
		Hygeia-O-Matic	Bladder	50		Low
		In-House Outhouse	Bladder	50		Low
		Flush Force	Bladder	70		Low
Tombstone/Urn						
	Mourn 1st 24 period					
		Tombstone/Urn	Bladder	5		Low
		Tombstone/Urn	Comfort	50		Low
		Tombstone/Urn	Energy	5		Low
		Tombstone/Urn	Fun	50		Low
		Tombstone/Urn	Hunger	5		Low
		Tombstone/Urn	Hygiene	50		Low
		Tombstone/Urn	Social	50		Low
		Tombstone/Urn	Room	50		Low
	Mourn 2nd 48 hours					
		Tombstone/Urn	Bladder	0		Low
		Tombstone/Urn	Comfort	30		Low
		Tombstone/Urn	Energy	0		Low
		Tombstone/Urn	Fun	30		Low
		Tombstone/Urn	Hunger	0		Low
		Tombstone/Urn	Hygiene	30		Low
		Tombstone/Urn	Social	30		Low
		Tombstone/Urn	Room	30		Low
Toy Box						
	Play					
		Toy Box	Fun	55	Playful	Medium
		Train set large	Fun	40		Low
		Train set large	Social	40		Low

OBJECT TYPE	POSSIBLE INTERACTIONS	OBJECT VARIATIONS	MOTIVE ADVERTISED	AD VALUE	PERSONALITY TRAIT MODIFIER	AD ATTENUATION
Train Set: Large						
	Play					
		Train set large	Fun	40		Medium
	Watch					
		Train set large	Fun	40		Low
		Train set large	Social	40		Low
Train Set: Small						
	Play					
		Train set small	Fun	45	Playful	Medium
	Watch					
		Train set small	Fun	20		Medium
		Train set small	Social	30		Medium
Trash Can: Inside						
	Empty trash					
		Trash Can Inside	Room	30	Neat	Medium
Trash Compactor						
	Empty trash					
		Trash Compactor	Room	30		High
Trash Pile						
	Clean					
		Trash Pile	Room	75	Neat	Medium
Tub						
	Clean					
		All Tubs	Room	20	Neat	High
	Take bath					
		Justa	Hygiene	50	Neat	Medium
		Justa	Comfort	20		Medium
		Sani-Queen	Hygiene	60	Neat	Medium
		Sani-Queen	Comfort	25		Medium
		Suds du Solei	Hygiene	65	Neat	Medium
		Suds du Solei	Comfort	28		Medium
		Hydrothera	Hygiene	70	Neat	Medium
		Hydrothera	Comfort	30		Medium
TV						
	Join					
		Monochrome	Fun	20	Lazy	High
		Trottco	Fun	30	Lazy	High
		Soma Plasma	Fun	45	Lazy	High
	Turn Off					
		All TVs	Energy	220	Neat	Medium

Object Type	Possible Interactions	Object Variations	Motive Advertised	Ad Value	Personality Trait Modifier	Ad Attenuation
TV, continued						
	Turn On					
		Monochrome	Fun	18	Lazy	High
		Trottco	Fun	35	Lazy	High
		Soma Plasma	Fun	49	Lazy	High
	Watch TV					
		Monochrome	Fun	18	Lazy	High
		Trottco	Fun	28	Lazy	High
		Soma Plasma	Fun	42	Lazy	High
VR Headset						
	Play					
		VR Headset	Fun	60	Playful	High

5
Social
Interactions

You *did* read the game manual, didn't you? Good. Because as we mentioned elsewhere, this guide assumes you know how the basic game interface works; you've maybe played *The Sims*, maybe a lot. You know how to direct a Sim's actions: click on an object or on another Sim to bring up a menu of actions you can perform. The manual calls this a "pie menu."

This chapter focuses on those menu choices. We call these *social interactions*. Why? Because we feel like it. Well, maybe there's another reason. But we're not going to tell you because our Mood is low and our Fun motive is bottoming out. So our pie menu includes the interaction "Tease."

See? We just had a social interaction. Life is indeed very much like *The Sims*.

> **TIP**
>
> Start each new house-hold with at least two Sims who can keep each other's Social motive score up. This is particularly true for Sims with a high Outgoing trait. Living alone, Outgoing Sims are hard-pressed to satisfy their powerful Social needs.

The Relationship Score

Good relationships are important to a Sim's ongoing struggle to get ahead. One primary objective in *The Sims* is to raise Relationship scores past the 50-point mark (the "friend-ship threshold") with as many Sim neighbors as possible. The more friends you make, the higher you can climb on your career ladder.

Fig. 5-1. Here, Bob Weigel needs more family friends. Work on getting his relationships with people outside the family above 50 points.

Sure, it's fun to slap folks. Slapping, teasing, bragging, scaring, insulting— you can indulge your dark side freely in *The Sims*, too. What a great game! But of course, you won't make many friends that way. Real life is like that too, I think.

For more about friends and careers (and a list of how many friends you need for each job promotion), refer to chapter 6, "Careers and Skills." For now, let's just say friends in *The Sims* are more than just friends. They're rungs in the career ladder.

Daily Relationship Decay

Relationships decay 2 points on both sides every day, whether the other Sim lives in your house or not. When a Sim's Relationship score with a friend falls close to 50, the friend calls to say, "We need to see each other more often."

Tips from the Testers

When trying to build friendships, avoid letting Sims choose their own social interactions with other Sims. They often make horrible decisions. The best way to build a good relationship with another Sim quickly: talk until the Relationship score hits 30. Compliment until 60. Hug until 100.

Avoid activating the "love bit," however. Don't kiss other Sims unless you're really looking for a mate. Love can slow the friend-making process because it provokes jealousy. Just make friends and send them on their way.

—Andrew Blomquist, Tester

Influence of Mood and Personality

A Sim's Playful, Nice, and Outgoing personality settings influence the interactions they choose. Consult the astrological signs for clues about which Sims get along and which will clash. (For more on this, see "Sim Zodiac Signs" in chapter 2, "Personality.") Sims in a bad mood, however, are very likely to have negative social interactions regardless of their personality traits. If either Sim engaged in a one-on-one social interaction—talking, joking, and so on—is in a bad mood, that interaction is more likely to have a negative outcome.

Topics of Conversation

Talk interests are ingrained. Different Sims have different interests. There is one exception to this rule, however. An adult will "map" his/her talk topics to match those of a kid. (For more on this, read on about Kid/Adult Conversations.) Sims with similar interests are likely to have very rewarding conversations. Keep an eye on the topic icons that appear in the talk bubbles above the heads of conversing Sims. Keep track of which neighbors share common interests.

Fig. 5-2. Keep an eye on those talk bubbles above Sims' heads. They reveal topics of interest and disinterest.

NOTE
Unless they're talking while they do something else (such as watching TV or eating—see "Group Talk" later in this section), Sims can talk to each other only one-on-one.

There are 12 general conversation topics in *The Sims*. Four are adult-only, four are kid-only, and four are available to both kids and adults. Every Sim has a high, medium, or low interest level (based on a scale of 1 to 10) in each conversation topic. These interest levels are assigned arbitrarily when a character is created and they never change.

TIP

While Sims sleep, their dream balloons display their unique set of high-interest conversation topics.

The Conversation Icons

Again, there are specific topics for adults and kids, as well as topics shared by both. Each conversation topic has three icons to represent it.

Adult-Only Topics

Money

Travel

Politics

'60s Stuff

Kid-Only Topics

Toys

Aliens

Pets

School

Adult/Kid Topics

Weather

Sports

Music

Outdoors

How Sim Conversations Work

The person who initiates a conversation always leads with a high-interest topic. A conversation is capped at four back-and-forth volleys of talk, but may end before that point due to low interest. Whether the conversation continues depends on each listener's interest level in the topic being discussed:

- A listener with high interest in the previous topic will continue talking about it.
- An even chance exists that a listener with medium interest in the previous topic will either continue discussing the same topic or change the subject.
- A 10 percent chance exists that a listener with low interest in the previous topic will continue on the same topic, a 40 percent chance the listener will change subjects, and a 50 percent chance the listener will exit the conversation.

A listener with a high interest in the topic will randomly display one of the topic's three icons. A listener with low interest in the topic, or one who changes the subject, displays an X balloon—a talk balloon showing the topic's icon with an X through it.

Fig. 5-3. This conversation got off on the wrong foot. Bob led with a remark about Flower Power in the '60s. But despite his hippie appearance, Biff isn't interested in the topic.

How Conversations Are Scored

There is a Relationship effect and a Social motive effect for the listener in each talk volley. A listener who likes the topic gets 5 Social points and 3 Relationship points. A listener who dislikes the topic gets 3 Social points and –3 Relationship points. In other words, even low interest can raise a Sim's Social motive in a Talk interaction.

Kid/Adult Conversations

Kids starting a conversation with an adult will bring up a kid-only or shared topic. Kids don't talk about adult topics, *ever*. Adults starting a conversation with a kid will bring up a kid-only or shared topic, as well. In this case, adult topics "map" to kid topics. That is, the adult's interest level in one of his or her own topics is applied to the kid topic.

Adult topics map to kid topics as follows:

ADULT TOPIC	CORRESPONDING KID TOPIC
Travel	Toys
Money	Aliens
Politics	Pets
'60s	School

Group Talk

When Sims talk while doing something else (such as watching TV or eating), they run a different kind of conversation algorithm, called Group Talk. *The Sims* take turns speaking about something of high interest to the speaker. (This is a good way to find out visitors' interests.) Speaking Sims get eight Social points and one Relationship point toward the Sim they're talking to—that is, the Sim in the group who responds to them.

Fig. 5-4. Group activities that offer Group Talk opportunities are classic "win-win" situations. Everybody gets positive Social and Relationship points, regardless of interests or personal feelings toward other participants.

Fig. 5-5. Some Group Talk objects (such as the §6,500 hot tub) are expensive. But a simple meal together triggers Group Talk, too.

NOTE

Group Talk uses only the four shared (adult/kid) topics—Weather, Sports, Music, and Outdoors.

In Group Talk, Sims may disagree but there is no relationship loss. They also don't have to worry about matching topics with each other. (They'll only discuss Kid/Adult topics, never Kid-only or Adult-only topics.) Thus, group activities present nice, safe ways to boost Social and Relationship scores without risking negative interaction. (See the corresponding tip from tester Syruss Flyte.)

Group Activities with Group Talk

Sims who join in the following activities take turns speaking to the group. Each speaker gains eight Social points and adds one Relationship point toward the Sim he or she is talking to—that is, the Sim who responds.

- Eat Group Meal
- Watch TV
- Hot tub
- Chessboard
- Large train set
- Dollhouse
- Pinball
- Pool table

Group Activities with No Group Talk

Some group activities don't feature Group Talk, with its automatic increase in Social and Relationship points. That doesn't mean such boosts aren't possible. In some cases, the activity offers random changes to your Sim's Social motive and/or Relationship score toward other participants.

Fig. 5-6. Dancing at the stereo is fun, and it guarantees random Group Talk gains in Social/Relationship areas.

- Basketball Hoop: Random Social/Relationship gain
- Piano/Guitar: Watchers can gain or lose both Social points and Relationship points toward player based on player's Creativity skill. Higher skill means more points gained; low skill can mean points lost.
- Stereo/Jukebox (Dance): Random Social/Relationship gain
- Play Structure: No Social/Relationship gain
- Swimming Pool: No Social/Relationship gain
- Vibromatic Bed (for two only): Random Relationship gain between participants, plus Fun/Social gain

Tips from the Testers

Sims with different sets of interests may find it hard to develop friendships, but Group Talk situations eliminate negative interactions. Use them to boost Relationship scores between incompatible Sims.

Prepare a Group Meal and eat, watch TV, crank up the model railroad set, play chess. Best of all, *use that hot tub!* When other Sims join the activity, your Sim's relationship with them goes up without any of the trouble that can come with regular social interactions.

—Syruss Flyte, Tester

Social Outcomes

A number of factors can influence social outcomes. In this section, we examine these factors, and include a point table that shows exactly how each potential outcome affects Social and Relationship scores. But first, let's talk about how to resurrect a deteriorating social life, and then take a quick peek at a couple of special social interactions that can trigger far-reaching outcomes.

When Social Life Goes Sour: How to Avoid the Downward Spiral

Most social interactions have more than one possible outcome. Mood, Motive levels, personality type, Relationship scores, and other factors influence that outcome. In turn, the outcome (good, bad, or indifferent) affects Social and Relationship scores, those twin indicators of social health.

Thus, if things start going bad, your Sim can get caught in a downward social spiral. Bad scores trigger bad interactions, which in turn send scores south still further. In fact, it can be very, very difficult to salvage any relationship, much less a bad one, with your Social score mired in the red. Here's our advice on escaping this trap. First, fill your house with group activity objects that trigger the automatic Group Talk interaction. (See "Group Talk" earlier in this chapter.) Again, Group Talk situations eliminate negative interactions. Even Sims that hate you will get a positive social buzz from a soak in the hot tub.

Fig. 5-7. If your Social/Relationship scores are buried in the red, load up on objects that offer Group Talk interactions.

Second, avoid one-on-one interactions with other Sims until you've raised your Social score to at least 0, preferably higher. After that, limit your social choices to Talk. Talking may trigger negative outcomes, but the risk is minimized. Keep talking and arranging Group Talk activities until your Social and Relationship scores climb back into a good green range.

Jealousy

Jealousy is a bad thing. It slaughters the Social motive, big time. Let's say Sim Betty loves Sim Bob. Both are in the same room. If Sim Jezebel enters and tries to engage in a dicey interaction (see the following list) with Bob, Betty will get jealous.

If Betty gets jealous, look out. She crosses her arms for a moment. Her Social score drops like a rock. Then she'll likely slap the snot out of Jezebel, flushing the harlot's Social scores right down the tubes, too.

The four interactions that can induce jealousy are:

- Kiss
- Hug
- Flirt
- Give Backrub

Fig. 5-8. Jealousy decimates a Sim's Social motive score. Plus, it triggers bad social interactions—like this impending slap fest, for example.

Attack

Sims can be vicious, given certain circumstances. A jealous or grouchy Sim can manifest dark feelings by attacking another Sim. Dust flies, smoke clears, and there's the loser, humiliated on the floor, with the winner crowing above.

Fortunately, strict rules govern this sort of Neanderthal behavior. Adults can attack other adults, but never kids. Kids can attack other kids, but not adults. Fights are moderated by the Nice personality trait. A very nice Sim will almost never attack, while a not-so-nice Sim (one with a Nice score of zero) is much more likely to. Adults might decide to move out of the house if attacked by a family member (25 percent chance), but kids won't. Any visitor who ends up on the losing end of an attack will leave the house immediately.

Fig. 5-9. Careful. Attacks between family members can drive the loser out of the game.

Limits to Social Interaction

Not all interactions are available for all Sim types. Kids, in particular, can't engage in actions such as Kiss, Flirt, Compliment, and Slap. Adults, on the other hand, can't play Tag, doggone it. The following table lists the possible combinations.

POSSIBLE ADULT/CHILD INTERACTIONS

INTERACTION	ADULT TO ADULT	KID TO KID	ADULT TO KID	KID TO ADULT
Kiss	X	—	—	—
Hug	X	X	X	X
Flirt	X	—	—	—
Give Backrub	X	—	—	—
Compliment	X	—	—	—
Cheer Up	X	X	X	X
Dance	X	—	—	—
Entertain	X	X	X	X
Give Gift	X	X	X	X
Joke	X	X	X	X
Talk	X	X	X	X
Call Here	X	X	X	X
Tickle	X	X	X	X
Brag	X	X	X	X
Insult	X	X	X	X
Slap	X	—	—	—
Scare	X	X	X	X
Tease	X	X	X	X
Attack	X	X	—	—
Apologize	X	—	—	—
Tag	—	X	—	—
Say Goodbye	X	X	X	—

Factors that Influence Social Outcomes

Every social interaction carries "baggage." When a Sim talks to another Sim, the outcome is affected by age (adult or child), sex, mood, individual personality traits, and other aspects of their relationship. Are they friends? Are they in love? Are their Social needs high or low?

All these things influence available pie menu choices and the outcome of selected interactions. In the table below, we list the factors that influence the outcome of various types of social interaction.

rel = Relationship	rom = romance flag
out = Outgoing	age = adult/child
play = Playful	social = Social motive value
ff = friend flag	vis = visitor
ss = same sex	budget = household budget

SOCIAL OUTCOME FACTORS

INTERACTION	FACTORS THAT DETERMINE APPEARANCE ON MENU	FACTORS THAT DETERMINE OUTCOME
Cheer Up	ff, mood (of friend), nice	rel
Kiss	ss, mood, rel, age	rel, mood, ss
Dance	age, mood, out, rel	rel, out, mood
Backrub	age, nice, mood, rel, out, ss	rel, out, ss
Flirt	age, social, ss, out, mood, rel, rom	rel, mood, ss
Gift	vis, budget, nice, mood, rel	rel, mood
Hug	age, out, mood, rel, ss	rel, out, mood, ss
Entertain	social, out, play, mood, rel	play, rel
Compliment	age, nice, out, mood, rel	rel, mood
Joke	play, mood, rel	play, mood, rel
Talk	mood, rel, out	topics match
Brag	nice, out, social, rel	rel, mood
Tease	nice, mood, rel	rel, mood
Tickle	social, out, play, active, mood, rel	rel, play
Insult	nice, mood, rel	nice
Slap	age, nice, mood, rel	nice, mood
Apologize	rel	mood
Scare	nice, mood, play, rel	play, mood
Attack	age, nice, mood, rel	body

How Social Interactions Are Scored

We've talked about how various factors can affect the outcomes of social interactions. Once those outcomes are triggered, your Sim's Social and Relationship scores change. Naturally, different outcomes have different effects on these scores.

The table that follows illustrates how each outcome of each possible social interaction affects Relationship and Social scores. In general, note that social interactions rarely have a negative effect on the Social motive. Bad outcomes usually score 0 Social points, at worst, and can even result in positive Social points. Apparently, bad social contact is better than no contact at all.

NOTE

In the following table, "Relationship Change" refers to the change in score toward the Sim's partner in the listed interaction.

EFFECTS OF OUTCOMES ON SOCIAL/RELATIONSHIP SCORES FOR INITIATOR AND RECEIVER

INTERACTION	RESPONSE	RELATIONSHIP CHANGE	SOCIAL SCORE CHANGE
Attack	Win Fight	−5	10
Attack	Lose Fight	−10	−20
Give Back Rub	Good	5	7
Give Back Rub	Bad	−7	0
Receive Back Rub	Good	9	13
Receive Back Rub	Bad	−10	0
Cheer Up	Good	5	7
Cheer Up	Neutral	0	5
Cheer Up	Bad	−3	0
Be Cheered Up	Good	10	10
Be Cheered Up	Neutral	0	5
Be Cheered Up	Bad	−10	0
Hug	Good	7	15
Hug	Tentative	2	7
Hug	Refuse	−10	0
Be Hugged	Good	8	15
Be Hugged	Tentative	4	7
Be Hugged	Refuse	−10	0
Flirt	Good	5	13
Flirt	Ignore	−5	0
Flirt	Refuse	−10	−17
Be Flirted With	Good	10	13
Be Flirted With	Ignore	0	0

EFFECTS OF OUTCOMES ON SOCIAL/RELATIONSHIP SCORES FOR INITIATOR AND RECEIVER, continued

INTERACTION	RESPONSE	RELATIONSHIP CHANGE	SOCIAL SCORE CHANGE
Be Flirted With	Refuse	−10	0
Compliment	Accept	5	5
Compliment	Reject	−10	0
Be Complimented	Accept	5	11
Be Complimented	Reject	−7	0
Give Gift	Accept	5	7
Give Gift	Stomp	−15	0
Receive Gift	Accept	10	13
Receive Gift	Stomp	−5	0
Insult	Cry	5	0
Insult	Stoic	0	3
Insult	Angry	−10	7
Be Insulted	Cry	−12	−13
Be Insulted	Stoic	−5	−5
Be Insulted	Angry	−14	−7
Slap	Cry	0	3
Slap	Slap Back	−10	−7
Be Slapped	Cry	−20	−17
Be Slapped	Slap Back	−15	7
Tease	Giggle	5	7
Tease	Cry	−4	0
Be Teased	Giggle	5	7
Be Teased	Cry	−13	−7
Scare	Laugh	5	10
Scare	Angry	−5	0
Be Scared	Laugh	5	8
Be Scared	Angry	−10	0
Talk	High Interest Topic	3	5
Talk	Like Topic	3	5
Talk	Dislike Topic	−3	3
Talk	Hate Topic	−3	3
Group Talk	N/A	1	8

INTERACTION	RESPONSE	RELATIONSHIP CHANGE	SOCIAL SCORE CHANGE
Dance	Accept	8	13
Dance	Refuse	−5	0
Be Danced With	Accept	10	13
Be Danced With	Refuse	−5	0
Tickle	Accept	5	13
Tickle	Refuse	−5	0
Be Tickled	Accept	8	13
Be Tickled	Refuse	−8	0
Brag	Good	5	13
Brag	Bad	−5	0
Be Bragged To	Good	5	7
Be Bragged To	Bad	−5	0
Joke	Laugh	5	13
Joke	Giggle	2	7
Joke	Uninterested	−6	0
Listen to Joke	Laugh	7	13
Listen to Joke	Giggle	3	7
Listen to Joke	Uninterested	−7	0
Entertain	Laugh	4	7
Entertain	Boo	−15	0
Be Entertained	Laugh	8	13
Be Entertained	Boo	−7	0
Apologize	Accept	10	15
Apologize	Reject	−10	0
Be Apologized To	Accept	10	15
Be Apologized To	Reject	−10	0
Kiss	Passion	12	20
Kiss	Polite	5	10
Kiss	Deny	−15	5
Be Kissed	Passion	12	20
Be Kissed	Polite	5	10
Be Kissed	Deny	−10	0

Friendship

Friendship is a key state in *The Sims*. Job advancement is impossible without building a network of neighborhood friends. (See chapter 6, "Careers and Skills" for details on this.) Two Sims don't become "friends" until both have a relationship to each other of at least 50. When this happens, you see that little blue smiley face appear below each other's picture in the Relationships subpanel and above their heads on the game screen.

Fig. 5-10. One of your biggest goals in THE SIMS is to grow the number circled here—your Family Friend Count. With only two friends, this family has a lot of work to do.

> NOTE
>
> The key number in a friendship is 50. To be friends, each Sim must have a 50 Relationship score with the other. If either score drops below 50, the friend-ship ends.

Friendships are two-way streets, though. If the relationship of either Sim toward the other drops below 50, the blue face disappears and the friendship ends—at least, until you repair it with some good socializing. Fortunately, friends warn you via phone when their score falls near 50.

> TIP
>
> Remember, the decay rate for all Relationship scores is 2 points per day. If Sims don't spend regular time with a friend, the relationship eventually fades below the friendship threshold.

The Genie's "Friend" Spell

The Antique Lamp's genie, added in the *Livin' Large* expansion pack, gives his Sim summoners random opportunities to choose a "Friends/Family" spell. If you choose Friends, the spell's outcome has a chance of being either good or bad. If good, the genie gives a hefty boost to the Relationship score between the Sim and a random acquaintance, and he also raises both Sims' motives to 70. This usually leads to instant friendship.

The bad outcome, as you might imagine, is just the opposite, pushing down both Relationship scores and various motive scores—which often leads to bad moods and boorish behavior. For more on the genie's spells, see "How the Genie Works" in chapter 9, "Sim Objects."

The Romance Bit

Unlike real-life love, where everything is always perfectly equal, romance in *The Sims* can be one-sided. If your Sim develops at least a 70 Relationship with another Sim, and then performs a "romantic interaction" (Hug, Kiss, Flirt, Give Backrub) with him or her, your Sim will likely fall in love. Or, in programmer-speak, "their romance bit will get set." Only then will the pie menu give your Sim the choice to Propose.

Remember, though—unlike friendship, love can be a one-way transaction.

Fig. 5-11. Ah, romance. To raise the relationship with your love-target above 70, try a few romantic interactions—Hug, Backrub, Flirt, Kiss—and sooner or later you'll score a heart.

TIP

Love can be lucrative! A good strategy for quickly increasing funds is to persuade neighbors who live alone to marry you or move in. If they say yes, their net worth is added to yours.

Propose/Move In

Flowchart time! Will Wright handed us the following chart scribbled in pencil on ugly graph paper. It describes how *The Sims* processes the act of proposing to a prospective mate. Marketing studies, however, indicate that consumers buy strategy guides almost entirely based on the aesthetic beauty of flow charts. So we took Will's pathetic scribble, digitally enhanced it, and then added immeasurable graphic nuance. Now buy this book.

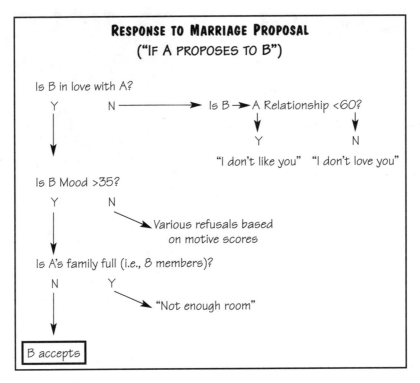

RESPONSE TO MARRIAGE PROPOSAL

("IF A PROPOSES TO B")

Is B in love with A?

Y   N   →   Is B → A Relationship <60?

                                          Y   N

                                 "I don't like you"   "I don't love you"

Is B Mood >35?

Y   N

                 → Various refusals based
                      on motive scores

Is A's family full (i.e., 8 members)?

N   Y

                → "Not enough room"

B accepts

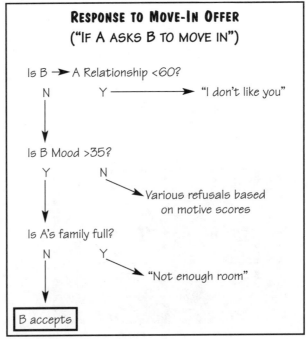

RESPONSE TO MOVE-IN OFFER

("IF A ASKS B TO MOVE IN")

Is B → A Relationship <60?

N   Y   →   "I don't like you"

Is B Mood >35?

Y   N

             → Various refusals based
                on motive scores

Is A's family full?

N   Y

          → "Not enough room"

B accepts

Weddings

The nuptial ceremony takes place automatically when one Sim accepts another's marriage proposal. Don't blink. It happens pretty fast. Then the new spouse brings a job and income into the household. If the spouse was the only adult in the previous home, the new partner brings his or her net worth . . . and kids, if any. (This leaves the ex-house empty and up for sale.) Interestingly, if a marrying Sim has kids, and another adult (a suffering ex-spouse, perhaps) remains in the old house, the kids stay put. Hey, it's only fair. Didn't you ever read *Horton Hatches an Egg*?

Fig. 5-12. OK, it sounds crass, but the best thing about weddings is the additional income a marriage brings into your household. Now you can buy some REALLY good stuff.

LIVIN' LARGE Love Aids

The *Livin' Large* expansion pack adds a couple of catalog items that can kick start a stagnant love life. Sims using the "Concatenation Station" Home Chemistry Set make one of eight random potions. The red one is the Love Potion; when drunk, it causes the drinker and his/her lowest-rated acquaintance (based on Relationship scores) of the opposite gender to fall in love.

The Antique Lamp's genie can cast a Love spell that has a 40/60 chance of good or bad outcomes. The good outcome causes the Sim summoner and his/her highest-rated non-lover (based on Relationship scores) to fall in love (gender depends on user's choice).

Family and Housemates

Family can be the warm, cozy hearth of *The Sims*. If you create Sim families with nice, outgoing personalities and guide them into similar schedules—eating and watching TV at the same time, for example—then families can do a pretty good job of taking care of their own social needs without micromanagement.

Tips from the Testers

A two-member family is the best way to keep up your Sims' Social motive score. Add a third member to manage household chores and procure friends so your other two Sims can focus on skill-building and maintaining a positive mood.

—Ed O'Tey, Tester

Sleeping with Housemates

Just because two Sims live together doesn't mean they like each other well enough to share a bed. If Sims won't sleep together, you'll have to improve their relationship to the Friendship level (50 points or higher) to get them both sleeping in the same bed at the same time. This doesn't apply to children, however. Children can sleep with a fellow household adult or child regardless of Relationship scores. Sims don't have to be of different genders or in love to share a bed. But they do have to be friends.

Fig. 5-13. This man won't sleep with that woman in the bed because they're not "friends." Know many guys like that?

LIVIN' LARGE in the Vibromatic Bed

The expansion pack adds a new bed with some very interesting new interactions. The Vibromatic Heart Bed not only lets you "Vibrate," but also allows consenting lovers to "Play in Bed." This act can boost Fun, Social, and Relationship totals, but it also sports a one-in-eight chance of producing a baby.

Babies

In all, *The Sims: Livin' Large* offers three ways to produce a baby. We've already mentioned the "Vibromatic way." Second, whenever two household members of the opposite sex kiss with passion, they trigger a one in five chance the game will offer them a baby. (We're glad the process is a bit more complicated in real life.) And third, if two adults in love live together in a house, there's a random chance of getting a phone offer to adopt a baby. If you choose to accept, the little bundle of joy appears in its crib, ready to be fed, played with, and sung to for three days. (Changing diapers, thank-

Fig. 5-14. Baby demands can wreak havoc on a household for the three days of their Sim infancy. Keep babies fed and sing them to sleep to minimize the time crunch.

fully, isn't an option.) The baby's gender is randomly assigned, and its personality based on the parents' personality. After three days, the baby morphs into a full-grown kid.

You can move cribs, but you can't delete them. Sims don't autonomously care for (Feed or Sing To) a baby. But they will choose to play with it. Both family members and visitors can interact with the baby, which is a "special object" with just two motives— Hunger and Energy. As these motives decrease, the baby cries. Crying babies wake up sleeping adults (but not kids) in the same room.

The Baby Ratings

Each of the baby motives—Hunger and Energy—has a rating from 0 to 2. Each motive decreases by 1 every two hours, except when the baby is sleeping. Playing with or singing to a baby raises its Energy score; feeding raises its Hunger score. (Duh!)

- 2 Energy/Hunger means the baby is fully rested/fed and doesn't cry.
- 1 Energy/Hunger means the baby is slightly tired/hungry and snuffles a small cry.
- 0 Energy/Hunger score means the baby desperately needs to sleep/eat. Baby makes a shrill, insistent cry.

Sleeping Babies

Sim babies can sleep only when their Hunger rating is above 0. Once asleep, a baby continues sleeping for six hours. While the baby sleeps, its Hunger score won't drop below 1; Hunger can fall below 1 only after baby wakes up. Sleeping returns Energy level to 2.

TIP

Your primary baby-care goal: *Get them to sleep.* Otherwise, they require constant care. Yes, playing with baby might be fun, but it's also very time-consuming.

Interacting with Babies

If a baby is quiet, you know both its needs are satisfied. But if a baby cries, you can't be sure whether Hunger or Energy is low. Best bet: feed the baby first. If Hunger reaches 0 while you playfully bounce the baby like an idiot, you risk losing the baby to Child Protective Services. (More on this in a minute.)

If the baby cries quietly, one or both of the motives must be at 1 (and no lower). Feed the baby first. If the crying doesn't stop, you know the Energy rating must be at 1. Now choose Sing. Singing puts the baby to sleep for six hours, which raises Energy to 2. (Choosing Play also raises Energy to 2, but it keeps the baby awake, which means its motives drop again in just two hours.)

TIP

If a baby continues crying during the interaction you've chosen, your choice isn't raising the baby's low motive. Remember, babies have only two needs. Try an interaction to satisfy the other need.

A shrill cry tells you one of the baby's motives is at 0. Feed it first—and hurry! If that doesn't work, the baby's Energy must be at 0. Playing has no effect on an overtired baby. Only singing works. Again, the Sing interaction puts the baby to sleep for six hours, returning its Energy to 2.

Losing Babies

If baby's Hunger rating goes to 0 for more than 60 Sim-minutes—well, sorry, this is a failure state, and you win the Joan Crawford "Mommy Dearest" Award. An unflappable Social Worker arrives and takes the baby. This sad episode can happen anytime (day or night) during the three-day babyhood period.

Kids

If a baby survives for three days after birth, he or she breaks out of the crib, stretches, and becomes a full-fledged, fun-loving Sim kid. Of course, you can add kids to your household right from the start in the Create a Family screen. Either way, you now face a daunting new challenge—Parenthood.

Fig. 5-15. This Social Worker means business. If you don't want to lose your baby, keep it fed.

Fig. 5-16. This Mom has "too many Daves." But hey, seven Daves means a seventy percent tax cut.

NOTE

Kids can save you money. You get a 10 percent "tax credit" on bills for each child in the household.

Attributes: Baby-to-Kid

A kid is a fully functioning Sim, with all eight motives working and a full set of talk interests. If you crafted your own kid at the Create a Sim screen, you allocated personality traits and *The Sims* assigned a random set of talk interests. But what happens if a kid comes into the world via babyhood?

Oddly, a Sim child "inherits" traits and interests from either mother or father, or from an average of both parents. Who would think up a cockamamie system like that? Skills are preset to a random amount; kids can't increase skills during the game. Kid skill values determine only how well they play piano, paint, or play basketball.

Kids and School

If a kid misses a day of school, his or her Report Card grade drops a whole grade point—for example, from B+ to C+. Kids can bring grades up by going to school in a good mood, or by selecting Study for School at a bookshelf or computer. Using the Horrorwitz telescope available in the *Livin' Large* expansion pack also counts as a Study activity for kids.

If a Sim child's grade drops to F and stays there for three days, the kid must go to Military School. If that happens, the family account is charged a one-time fee of §1,000. Ouch! Worse, your deadbeat kid leaves the household and disappears into SimSpace, never to return.

Kids and Social Interactions

The Possible Adult/Child Interactions table earlier in this chapter shows which interactions are available to Sim kids. As you might expect, kids are limited in their object interactions, as well. No stiff drinks at the bar. No cooking or lighting fires.

> **NOTE**
> Fun matters more to kids. It plays a bigger part in their mood and drains quickly. So kids have to do fun stuff a lot.

Visitors

Visitors are neighbors. And neighbors, unless you import families or keep the Newbies and Goths, are Sims you created and placed in the neighborhood. Keep that in mind if they exasperate the Sims in your current household. It's your fault.

> **TIP**
> Always keep a group platter of food available for neighbors who drop by. First thing home from work—hit the fridge and Serve Dinner. Then take care of basic needs, such as Bladder or Hygiene, to be in the best mood possible when visitors arrive.

Visitor Motives and Intelligence

Actually, visitors are somewhat "smarter" than your current family members. That is, they take care of their own needs better. When presented with choices, visitors always pick the interaction with the highest happiness contribution value (the one that will improve their mood the most).

But neighbors are polite. They won't raid your fridge if they're hungry, for example, or shoot a game of pool without an invitation. Instead, they go home. So if you want to keep your visitors around long enough to make friends, you must provide them with opportunities to satisfy certain needs. (See "Keeping Neighbors Happy.")

Fig. 5-17. Keep a group platter of food on the table for visitors. They often arrive hungry.

> **TIP**
>
> Buy a phone immediately. A phone allows Sims to invite visitors and order services. But your Sims can call only folks they've already met, so be sure to greet neighbors when they drop by.

Greeting Visitors

Each neighbor has an equal likelihood of visiting. Visitors ring the doorbell and wait to be greeted. If one of your family Sims doesn't greet the visitor within one Sim-hour, the neighbor strolls back home. Your most interruptible family member (that is, anyone idling) will answer the door; only one family member greets the visitor.

The type of greeting depends on your Sim's relationship to the visitor. If they're in love with each other, they exchange a "polite" kiss. If they're friends, they hug briefly. In all other cases, they shake hands. Greeted visitors can move freely through the doorway and wander through the house.

Fig. 5-18. Sim visitors are remarkably patient, waiting an entire Sim-hour for you to answer the doorbell. If you don't greet them within that time, they head back home.

Neighbor Visit Schedule

Neighbors in *The Sims* are very, you know, *neighborly*. They like to drop by, see how you're doing, check out your stuff—er, your state of mind. And they do it with almost frightening regularity.

The Welcome Wagon

If neighbors exist on Sim Lane, one or two will drop by at 9:30 a.m. on the first day. *The Sims* does this to help jump-start your social life. Game designers can be so darned thoughtful.

Drop-Ins

If there are neighbors you haven't met, *The Sims* will sort through them each day at noon and 6 p.m. and decide whether to send one to visit you in "drop-in" fashion. Drop-ins come unannounced to your door. The more full houses in the neighborhood, the more likely the game will find someone to drop in on you.

Once you greet neighbors, however, they can no longer be selected to drop in. You must call neighbors you've met already to arrange visits.

Daily Walk-by

Sometimes your Sims can't greet drop-in visitors because they're at work or busy. But neighbors take daily walks around the Sim Lane block. At 10 a.m., 2 p.m., 4 p.m., and 8 p.m., the game selects a random neighbor to stroll the sidewalk past your house. These strollers walk directly off the lot unless one of your family members greets them first. You must direct this greeting, however. Family members never greet strolling neighbors autonomously.

Fig. 5-19. If you're having trouble meeting people, hang out on the sidewalk and intercept strollers. Neighbors walk by daily at 10 a.m., 2 p.m., 4 p.m., and 8 p.m.

Party Balloons

The *Livin' Large* expansion pack gives you a slick way to attract neighbors and induce them to stay longer. The "Party Balloons" catalog object is a bouquet of brightly colored balloons with truly "magnetic" properties. When you place them anywhere on your lot, Party Balloons have a 50 percent chance of generating a visitor *every half hour* until either all balloons have popped or five visitors have appeared. (One balloon pops every hour and 20 minutes.)

And that's not all. Party Balloons slow the decay rate of everyone's Comfort, Hygiene, Bladder, and Hunger motives. They also speed up the decay rate of the Social motive, which spurs every Sim on the premises to look for more social interaction.

Calling Neighbors

First of all, in a grand concession to reality, *The Sims* makes it impossible to call neighbors who don't have a phone. As *The Sims* manual points out a number of times, put a phone into every house before you do anything else. Without phones, Sims are hard to reach. Impossible, in fact.

Neighbors are more likely to respond positively to a phone invitation if they like the Sim who invites them (it's irrelevant how the caller feels). A neighbor who accepts an invitation has a 25 percent chance of asking permission to bring friends. (This is an option only if the neighbor actually *has* friends—that is, Sims with whom they have a 50 or higher Relationship score.) If you say yes, the neighbor may bring along as many as three more Sims.

> **NOTE**
> Sims don't hide their feelings well. When a Sim calls a neighbor, voices on either end of the phone reflect the quality of the relationship.

If you call neighbors between 1 and 6 a.m., they won't come over. No surprise there. If fact, they get real ornery and your Relationship with them decreases. If you call any Sim with whom your Relationship is under –50 they'll hang up on you. Finally, all Sim kids wisely refuse invitations after 7:30 p.m., no matter what.

Start Motives and Leave Conditions

When visitors arrive, their motives start out at the following values. For those with a range, the start value is randomly selected from within the range.

VISITOR'S STARTING MOTIVES

MOTIVE	STARTING VALUE
Bladder	0 to 30
Comfort	30 to 70
Energy	35
Fun	–20 to 20
Hunger	–30 to –20
Hygiene	90
Social	–50 to –40

Visitors go back home when the time passes 1 a.m. or any one of their motives falls below the critical values in the following table. If the latter happens, the exiting Sims' thought balloons indicate which motive caused them to leave.

VISITORS WILL LEAVE . . .

IF MOTIVE:	DROPS BELOW VALUE:
Energy	−80
Comfort	−70
Hunger	−50
Hygiene	−70
Bladder	−90
Social	−85
Fun	−55
Room	−100
Mood	−75

Keeping Visitors Happy

Yes, visitors are smart. If you give them good choices, they tend to make good decisions. But it's up to you to be a good host. Sure, talking is important to raise Social and Relationship scores. But if you focus on social interactions only, your visitors will leave when other motives fall below their critical values.

Fig. 5-20. Visitors arrive with their motive levels fairly low. Best be ready with activities to meet their needs—have the TV on, the food out, and so forth.

Keep group platters of food on the table for Hunger. For Fun, keep the TV and stereo blasting; hit the hot tub or pool to invite followers. Also important—let your guests wander off to do their own thing at times. They need to sit down and relax for Comfort, or use the bathroom for Bladder and Hygiene purposes.

TIP

Servo, the all-purpose robot available with the *Livin'* Large expansion pack, is particularly adept at scanning Sims to find low motives and then supplying whatever's needed to boost them. Therefore, Servo is not only the ultimate housemate; he's also a superb co-host to any guests you might entertain.

Activities Available to Visitors

Not all activities in your home are available to neighbors. Note three types:

Family Member –Enabled Activities

One of your family members must "prepare" these two interactions before a neighbor can partake. First, neighbors can't help themselves to food in the fridge. They can eat only a prepared meal. So before guests arrive, click on the fridge and Serve Dinner (or any meal appropriate to the time of day). Second, neighbors won't turn on your TV. So turn it on for them. Once you do, they can sit and watch.

Joinable Activities

Neighbors won't perform certain interactions until a family member does them first. A Sim who starts an activity can invite the visitor to join. (Just click on the visitor and select Join or its equivalent.) Neighbors may join these activities autonomously, if they need the motives offered.

JOINABLE ACTIVITIES

After "Host" Sim Uses Object	Activity Available to Visitors
Basketball Hoop	Join
Chess	Join
Dollhouse	Watch
Hot Tub	Join
Pinball Machine	Join
Play Structure	Join
Piano	Watch
Guitar	Watch
Pool Table	Join
Stereo	Join Dance
Train Set	Watch

Autonomous Activities

Neighbors can take care of their own needs, in many cases. The basic strategy: don't hog all their time. Give visitors a chance to grab a cup of coffee, use the toilet, or sit on the couch if they need it. Here's a list of the activities a visitor will engage in autonomously if left alone long enough to do so.

VISITORS' AUTONOMOUS ACTIVITIES

OBJECT	AUTONOMOUS ACTION
Aquarium	Watch Fish
Baby	Play
Bar	Have a drink
Chair	Sit
Chair (Recliner)	Sit
Espresso Machine	Drink Espresso
Coffeemaker	Drink Coffee
Fire	Panic
Flamingo	View
Fountain	Play
Love 'n Haight Lamp	View
Painting	View
Pool	Swim
Pool (Diving Board)	Dive In
Pool (Ladder)	Get In/Out
Sculpture	View
Sink	Wash Hands
Sofa	Sit
Toilet	Use, Flush
Tombstone/Urn	Mourn
Toy Box	Play
Trash Can (Inside)	Dispose

TIP

Give guests freedom to make some autonomous decisions. But always find time to interact with them, too. If you don't, visitors feel ignored and head home.

Ghosts

Sims can die. That's bad. If they die on your property, they create an urn (inside the house) or tombstone (outside the house). But departed Sims don't consider urns or tombstones to be sufficient memorials. In fact, they want to keep their icy fingers in your business.

So every night at 11 p.m., every urn and tombstone on your lot has a one in eight chance of spewing out the ghost of the dead Sim buried there. Then the ghosts haunt your house.

Fig. 5-21. Sims who die on your lot aren't completely gone. Each tombstone or urn can produce the spirit of the dearly departed at 11 o'clock each night.

How Ghosts Operate

Each ghost is a pale version of its predeath self. However, ghosts are invisible much of the time. They glide around the house making a ghostly sound. This is amusing, but it has a downside. The moaning wakes up adults (but not kids) sleeping in the same room. So it's really bad for healthy sleep patterns.

If a Sim is awake when the ghost enters the room, things get even more fun. The ghost remains invisible until it slips behind the Sim. Then it suddenly becomes visible and scares the poor Sim. The scared Sim's reaction is to panic and run away. If more than two Sims are awake in the room, the ghost will scare the closest. If no one in the room is awake, the ghost will wander around sadly for a while, then disappear.

Tips from the Testers

Ghosts won't climb stairs. If you have a two-story house, put your Sims' bedrooms on the second floor and keep urns on the ground floor. This keeps ghosts from awakening your Sims in the middle of the night.

—Syruss Flyte, Tester

Getting Rid of Ghosts

Ghosts are amusing. But, again, they can be annoying, too. Fortunately, they're pretty easy to exorcise. Ghosts are deleted if you delete their urn/tombstone or bulldoze the lot. If an urn is included among the objects in a house when a family is evicted, it gets sold with the rest of the stuff. However, if a tombstone is in the yard when a family is evicted, the tombstone remains (as if it were an architectural object).

6

Careers and Skills

Deadbeat families don't last long in *The Sims*. They may draw a lucky "chance card" here and there to keep them alive for a few more weeks, but sooner or later the food runs out and burial urns appear. Fortunately, jobs are easy to get, and career advancement is a large part of the fun in *The Sims*. It's an invigorating challenge to follow a career track to the top, make big bucks, and then buy a Large Black Slab for §12,648.

In this section we examine the game's career tracks and offer tips on job advancement. We cover skill-building, the key to getting ahead in any career. A comprehensive table at the end of the chapter lists requirements and benefits for all 10 jobs within each of the game's 15 career tracks—10 from the original game, plus 5 new tracks added by the *Livin' Large* expansion pack.

Careers

The original version of *The Sims* features 10 career tracks—Business, Entertainment, Law Enforcement, Life of Crime, Medicine, Military, Politics, Pro Athlete, Science, and Xtreme. The *Livin' Large* expansion pack adds five more—Musician, Slacker, Paranormal, Journalism, and Hacker.

Each career track has 10 positions, starting with low-paying flunky jobs, such as Waiter, Team Mascot, and Golf Caddy, and building up to top-level glamour gigs, such as Business Tycoon, Criminal Mastermind, and our personal favorite, Professional Party Guest.

The tables in "The 15 Career Tracks" provide a complete listing of salaries, work hours, skill requirements, and other information for every job in *The Sims*.

NOTE
Sims who change career tracks must start their new tracks at entry-level jobs. However, they keep all the skill points they've earned. Thus, job promotions in new tracks happen faster if the Sims are already skilled in the right areas.

Choosing a Career Track

As we pointed out in chapter 2, "Personality," having certain personality traits makes it easier to build certain skills. Therefore, the job you choose for each Sim should emphasize skills accelerated by that Sim's personality.

NOTE
Careers that require Body skill are the hardest to achieve promotions. Since body-improving activities drain Energy, these Sims end up having less time in the day to maintain motives and make friends.

Fig. 6-1. Personality traits increase the speed with which a Sim acquires corresponding skills. For example, outgoing types develop Charisma more quickly.

TIP

If the house you build keeps your Sims reasonably happy, you buy a little freedom. An efficient home and objects that satisfy basic Sim needs allow you to leave your game running autonomously without your Sims losing their jobs.

HOW TO MATCH CAREERS TO PERSONALITY

CAREER TRACK	NECESSARY SKILLS	CORRESPONDING PERSONALITY TRAITS
Business	Logic, Charisma	Outgoing
Entertainment	Charisma, Creativity	Outgoing, Playful
Law Enforcement	Logic, Body	Active
Life of Crime	Creativity, Charisma	Playful, Outgoing
Medicine	Logic, Body	Active
Military	Repair, Body	Active
Politics	Charisma, Logic	Outgoing
Pro Athlete	Body, Charisma	Active, Outgoing
Science	Logic, Creativity	Playful
Xtreme	Creativity, Body/Charisma (tie)	Playful, Active, Outgoing
Musician	Creativity, Charisma, Body	Playful, Outgoing, Active
Slacker	Mechanical, Charisma, Body	Outgoing, Active
Paranormal	Creativity, Charisma, Logic	Playful, Outgoing
Journalism	Creativity, Charisma, Logic	Playful, Outgoing
Hacker	Mechanical, Logic, Creativity, Charisma	Playful, Outgoing

Getting a Job

Sims never seek employment on their own. And if you order Sims to look for a job, they'll comply only if they're in a good mood.

Jobs are plentiful in the Sim world. But you'll find one (and only one) position posted in the newspaper every day. So here's a tip: if you desire a different career track from the one you see in the paper, you needn't wait for the next day's paper delivery, even if your funds are very limited. Instead, try the following trick.

When you first place your Sim family on a lot, don't buy anything until you check the newspaper for that day's job offer. If it's not the career you want, buy a cheap desk, chair, and computer. Do your job search on the computer, which offers *three* job choices instead of one. Take a job in your desired career track and then sell back the computer, desk, and chair.

If you return the equipment the same day you bought the items, you get a full refund, no depreciation. And, hey, if the three online job choices don't thrill you either, return the equipment anyway and repeat the purchase-seek-return trick the next day.

Fig. 6-2. Buy a desk, chair, and computer the minute you move a Sim family onto a new lot. A computer allows you to choose from THREE jobs. And, if money's tight, you can sell back the equipment for a full cash refund when you're done!

Job Performance

Mood is the key to job performance, which is updated daily. The game averages every working Sim's current mood with the previous day's performance rating. High mood ratings lead to promotions. Low ratings lead to demotions.

Promotion

Promotions are nice things. The salary boost is usually significant, and most promotions include a generous cash bonus. However, beginning with each track's Level 3 job, every hop up the career ladder requires a specific number of skills and family friends. Click your Sim's Job button in the Control Panel to view requirements for the next level. Regardless of mood, if your Sim doesn't meet these criteria, your Sim won't get promoted.

Fortunately, the first promotion in any career track (from Level 1 to Level 2) requires no specific friends or skills. Unless they're miserable, your Sims will find it easy to climb their careers' first rungs.

After a Sim builds enough skill and acquires enough friends to advance to the next job level, the random chance for promotion is skewed by daily job performance. In other words, the better the mood, the better the job performance, and thus the greater the odds for promotion. Thus, sending your Sims to work in a good mood (theirs, not yours) is important.

Do your best to fulfill all your Sims' needs before they go to work each day. Best bet: send your Sims to bed early so they can rise at least

Fig. 6-3. To get promoted, your Sims must build appropriate skills, make friends, and go to work in a good mood.

two hours before the car pool arrives the next morning. This gives you time to satisfy basic physical needs, such as Hunger, Bladder, and Hygiene (which degrade significantly during a full night's sleep), *before* they head to work.

Fig. 6-4. Get your Sims to bed early enough to get a full Energy boost, yet still have time in the morning to satisfy basic physical needs before work.

TIP

Good job performance alone isn't enough to climb the career ladder. Your Sims must hone the skills their jobs require. Check the Job Panel periodically to find out what the skills are and learn how to improve them.

Tips from the Testers

My favorite career track is the Military. It's high-paying in the early levels, so you get a great start, and you don't need to worry about making and maintaining friends until your Sim tries for the Level 6 position, Flight Officer. Entering the Military track is a great way for players new to *The Sims* to start out.

—Andrew Blomquist, Tester

Friend Requirement

Here's a happy fact. The friend requirement for a job promotion refers to "family friends"—that is, friends of your household. So if another Sim in your household has made a friend, that person counts as a family friend for you, too. You can see how a stay-at-home Sim who spends all day cooking, cleaning, and making neighborhood friends can greatly boost his/her working partner's climb up the career ladder.

Fellow household members don't count as family friends for purposes of job promotion, however. If two or more members of your Sim household share the same friend, that friend counts as a family friend only once.

Fig. 6-5. You can't get to the top in any career without plenty of family friends. Have your Sims socialize as much as possible.

Demotion

Poor job performance increases a Sim's risk for demotion. In fact, job performance is the *only* factor considered in demoting Sims at work. Missing a day of work here or there has no effect on job performance. Losing friends or skill is irrelevant, too. To prevent demotions, just send your Sims to work in a good mood.

Getting Fired

A Sim who misses work two days in a row gets sacked—no excuses, no arbitration, no severance package. Just a phone call—*good-bye*. This is the *only* way to get fired. (You can skip one day of work with no repercussions other than lost wages, unless you have a night job. With night jobs, you lose your job the first time you miss work.)

Unfortunately, getting fired knocks a Sim completely out of the current career track and back to square one. Any new position will be entry level, even if it's in the same career track as the job the Sim squandered.

Workday Motive Decay

When Sims are home, their need scores drop at a standard rate, modified somewhat by personality traits and living conditions. This standard motive decay is turned off, however, when the Sims are at work, replaced by a daily motive decay rate fixed for each job.

Every job affects motives in a different way. For example, Law Enforcement positions suffer far greater on-the-job Comfort decay than other careers (especially Captain Hero with his tight costume), yet somewhat less Hunger decay (all those donut stops, you know). Pro Athletes come home with spent Energy and Hygiene levels. Criminals and

Tips from the Testers

It's entirely possible for a Sim to go to work only every other day and still succeed. I wouldn't recommend this until your Sim gets a few promotions and a decent salary. But a Sim who reaches about Level 4 should find it relatively easy to get by working only every other day.

Use days off to build skills and make friends. As soon as you can afford skill-building equipment (chessboard, exercise machine, and so on), skip two days of work to get fired, and then focus on skills. Once you have skills, it's pretty easy to advance back up the career ladder. Job promotions are difficult to earn only when your Sim is just starting out and has no skills at all.

—Andrew Blomquist, Tester

Fig. 6-6. Let your Sims take a day off every few days to focus on building skills and making new friends.

Politicians return with lower Social scores. (Coincidence? We think not.) Military personnel suffer the biggest Fun drain. Apparently, getting shot at is kind of a drag.

Refer to the tables in "The 15 Career Tracks" section to learn the daily motive decay rates for each job.

Car Pool

Car pool vehicles arrive one hour before work starts and wait for an hour. (Starting times often differ for each job. Again, see "The 15 Career Tracks" tables.) Sims in a good mood go to work autonomously—that is, they don their work clothes and walk out to the car pool when it arrives. If they're in a bad mood, however, you must direct them to go to work. A worker leaving for the car pool with less than 15 minutes to spare will run to the vehicle.

Chance Cards

Career "chance cards" (dialog boxes describing some event that happened at work) come up periodically after work. These cards add or subtract skill points and/or money. Here's a frightening game fact: hitting Level 10 (the highest level) in any career gives your Sim a 1-in-20 chance of drawing a chance card that switches him or her to a lower level in another career!

Fig. 6-7. Don't go right to the car pool when it arrives! The car waits one hour, and your Sims can wait until the very last minute—literally. Use the time to boost motive scores or skills.

Tips from the Testers

Although the car pool may arrive at, say, 8 a.m., your Sim needn't *catch* it at 8 a.m. Don't waste an hour by jumping right into the car pool as soon as it arrives. As long as you've started routing your Sim to it by one minute before it leaves, the car pool will wait. Have your Sims build their motives during that hour so they have a successful day at work.

—Andrew Blomquist, Tester

CAUTION

Repairing appliances without calling a Repairman can be dangerous. Sims with low Mechanical skill can get electrocuted when fixing electronics. Hit the bookshelf and "Study Mechanical." Also, the better a Sim's Mechanical skill, the more quickly the Sim can repair broken objects. Naturally, the Repairman has the best Mechanical skill of all, but he charges $50 per hour.

Skill Building

Sims don't build skills autonomously. You must direct the little folks to better themselves. (Of course, Sims in a bad mood won't engage in any skill-building activity except to earn Body points in the pool.) Once a Sim earns a skill point by interacting with a particular skill-building object—say, playing piano or guitar for Creativity—the Sim may continue using that object until the mood rating drops below a certain value, causing an "exit condition." (See "Exit Conditions" in Chapter 4, "Sim Autonomy" for more info.)

Sims may engage in skill-building activities even after maxing out their skills. For example, a Sim with a Body skill rating of 10 can still work out on an exercise machine. Why you would inflict such punishment on an innocent Sim is between you and your conscience, however.

How to Improve Skills

Each succeeding skill point takes longer and longer to earn. A Sim may need to engage in a skill-building activity for only one hour to get the first skill point. Gaining the second skill point will take two hours, the third three hours, and so on.

The game manual lists the objects Sims must use to improve their skills. The following list includes a few notes about each.

SKILL	METHOD OF ENHANCEMENT	NOTES
Cooking	Bookshelf (Study Cooking)	Type of bookshelf (cheap or expensive) has no effect on skill activity.
Mechanical	Bookshelf (Study Mechanical)	Type of bookshelf (cheap or expensive) has no effect on skill activity.
Mechanical	Woodworking Table (Make Gnome)	Shy or Cranky Sims acquire skill more quickly.
Body	Exercise Machine (Work Out)	Exercise machine increases skill four times faster than the pool. Active Sims acquire skill more quickly.
Body	Pool (Swim)	Pool increases skill four times more slowly than the exercise machine. Active Sims acquire skill more quickly.
Charisma	Mirrors or Medicine Cabinet (Practice Speech)	Outgoing Sims acquire skill more quickly.
Creativity	Easel (Paint)	Playful Sims acquire skill more quickly.
Creativity	Piano, Guitar (Play)	Playful Sims acquire skill more quickly.
Logic	Chessboard (Play)	Playing chess with another Sim also nets you Social points
Logic	Home Chemistry Lab (Make Potion)	Drinking potions has wacky results.
Logic	Telescope (Gaze)	Random chance of being abducted by UFO.

CAUTION

A Sim cook without Cooking skill creates a fire hazard. Sims who know how to cook well also make more filling meals.

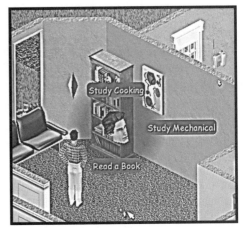

Fig. 6-8. A bookshelf, no matter how cheap, lets your Sims bone up on Cooking and Mechanical skills.

Tips from the Testers

Always buy a bookshelf right away. If money is tight, buy the cheapest one. Use bookshelves to raise Cooking skills to lower the risk of cooking fires and increase the value of cooked food. A Sim can study Maintenance skills, as well, to effectively eliminate the need to call the Repairman and fork over $50 per hour every time something breaks.

—Syruss Flyte, Tester

The 15 Career Tracks

The following tables list the salaries, hours, car pool vehicles, and job level requirements for the 15 career tracks available in *The Sims* and its expansion pack, *Livin' Large*. Also listed is the daily decay rate for each motive when the Sim is at work.

NOTE

All children go to school daily from 9 a.m. to 3 p.m. The school bus arrives at 8 a.m. and leaves by 9 a.m.

REQUIREMENTS FOR LEVEL 1 POSITIONS

Career Track	Position	Daily Pay	Hours	Car Pool Vehicle	Cooking	Repair	Charisma	Body	Logic	Creativity	Family Friends	Daily Motive Decay (Hunger/Comfort/ Hygiene/Bladder/ Energy/Fun/Social)
Business	Mail Room	§120	9 a.m.–3 p.m.	Junker	O	O	O	O	O	O	O	0/0/0/0/-30/0/0
Entertainment	Waiter/Waitress	§100	9 a.m.–3 p.m.	Junker	O	O	O	O	O	O	O	0/0/0/0/-30/0/0
Law Enforcement	Security Guard	§240	12 a.m.–6 a.m.	Squad Car	O	O	O	O	O	O	O	0/0/0/0/-30/0/0
Life of Crime	Pickpocket	§140	9 a.m.–3 p.m.	Junker	O	O	O	O	O	O	O	0/0/0/0/-30/0/0
Medicine	Medical Technician	§200	9 a.m.–3 p.m.	Junker	O	O	O	O	O	O	O	0/0/0/0/-30/0/0
Military	Recruit	§250	6 a.m.–12 p.m.	Military Jeep	O	O	O	O	O	O	O	0/0/-15/0/-30/0/0
Politics	Campaign Work	§220	9 a.m.–6 p.m.	Junker	O	O	O	O	O	O	O	0/0/0/0/-30/0/0
Pro Athlete	Team Mascot	§110	12 p.m.–6 p.m.	Junker	O	O	O	O	O	O	O	0/0/-5/0/-35/0/0
Science	Test Subject	§155	9 a.m.–3 p.m.	Junker	O	O	O	O	O	O	O	0/0/0/0/-30/0/0
Xtreme	Daredevil	§175	9 a.m.–3 p.m.	Junker	O	O	O	O	O	O	O	0/0/0/0/-30/0/0
Music	Subway Musician	§90	3 p.m.–8 p.m.	Junker	O	O	O	O	O	O	O	0/0/0/0/-30/0/0
Slacker	Golf Caddy	§90	5 a.m.–10 a.m.	Junker	O	O	O	O	O	O	O	0/0/0/0/-25/0/0
Paranormal	Psychic Phone Friend	§100	6 p.m.–12 a.m.	Junker	O	O	O	O	O	O	O	0/0/0/0/-24/0/0
Journalism	Typesetter	§120	4 a.m.–12 p.m.	Junker	O	O	O	O	O	O	O	0/0/0/0/-24/0/0
Hacker	Beta Tester	§120	9 a.m.–5 p.m.	Junker	O	O	O	O	O	O	O	0/0/0/0/-24/0/0

REQUIREMENTS FOR LEVEL 2 POSITIONS

Career Track	Position	Daily Pay	Hours	Car Pool Vehicle	Cooking	Repair	Charisma	Body	Logic	Creativity	Family Friends	Daily Motive Decay (Hunger/Comfort/ Hygiene/Bladder/ Energy/Fun/Social)
Business	Executive Assistant	§180	9 a.m.–4 p.m.	Junker	O	O	O	O	O	O	O	0/0/0/0/-34/-2/0
Entertainment	Extra	§150	9 a.m.–3 p.m.	Junker	O	O	O	O	O	O	O	0/0/0/0/-34/-2/0
Law Enforcement	Cadet	§320	9 a.m.–3 p.m.	Squad Car	O	O	O	O	O	O	O	0/0/0/0/-34/-2/0
Life of Crime	Bagman	§200	11 p.m.–7a.m.	Junker	O	O	O	O	O	O	O	0/0/0/0/-34/-2/0
Medicine	Paramedic	§275	11 p.m.–5a.m.	Junker	O	O	O	O	O	O	O	0/0/0/0/-34/-2/0
Military	Elite Forces	§325	7 a.m.–1 p.m.	Military Jeep	O	O	O	O	O	O	O	0/0/-15/0/-34/-2/0
Politics	Intern	§300	9 a.m.–3 p.m.	Junker	O	O	O	O	O	O	O	0/0/0/0/-34/-2/0
Pro Athlete	Minor Leaguer	§170	9 a.m.–3 p.m.	Junker	O	O	O	O	O	O	O	0/0/-10/0/-40/-2/0
Science	Lab Assistant	§230	11 p.m.–5a.m.	Junker	O	O	O	O	O	O	O	0/0/0/0/-34/-2/0
Xtreme	Bungee Jump Instructor	§250	9 a.m.–3 p.m.	Junker	O	O	O	O	O	O	O	0/0/0/0/-34/-2/0
Music	Piano Tuner	§120	9 a.m.–4 p.m.	Junker	O	O	O	O	O	O	O	0/0/0/0/-28/0/0
Slacker	Convenience Store Clerk	§110	10 p.m.–3 a.m.	Junker	O	O	O	O	O	O	O	0/0/0/0/-30/0/0
Paranormal	Conspiracy Theorist	§130	11 p.m.–5 a.m.	Junker	O	O	O	O	O	O	O	0/0/0/0/-30/0/0
Journalism	Game Reviewer	§200	11 a.m.–6 p.m.	Junker	O	O	O	O	O	O	O	0/0/0/0/-28/0/0
Hacker	Support Tech	§150	8 a.m.–4 p.m.	Junker	O	O	O	O	O	O	O	0/0/0/0/-24/0/0

REQUIREMENTS FOR LEVEL 3 POSITIONS

CAREER TRACK	POSITION	DAILY PAY	HOURS	CAR POOL VEHICLE	COOKING	REPAIR	CHARISMA	BODY	LOGIC	CREATIVITY	FAMILY FRIENDS	DAILY MOTIVE DECAY (HUNGER/COMFORT/ HYGIENE/BLADDER/ ENERGY/FUN/SOCIAL)
Business	Field Sales Rep	§250	9 a.m.–4 p.m.	Junker	0	2	0	0	0	0	0	-3/0/-5/0/-38/-4/0
Entertainment	Bit Player	§200	9 a.m.–3 p.m.	Junker	0	0	2	0	0	0	0	-3/0/-5/0/-38/-4/0
Law Enforcement	Patrol Officer	§380	5 p.m.–1a.m.	Squad Car	0	0	0	2	0	0	0	-3/0/-5/0/-38/-4/0
Life of Crime	Bookie	§275	12 p.m.–7 p.m.	Std. Car	0	0	0	2	0	0	0	-3/0/-5/0/-38/-4/0
Medicine	Nurse	§340	9 a.m.–3 p.m.	Std. Car	0	2	0	0	0	0	0	-3/0/-5/0/-38/-4/0
Military	Drill Instructor	§250	8 a.m.–2 p.m.	Military Jeep	0	0	0	2	0	0	0	-3/0/-20/0/-38/-4/0
Politics	Lobbyist	§360	9 a.m.–3 p.m.	Std. Car	0	0	2	0	0	0	0	-3/0/-5/0/-38/-4/0
Pro Athlete	Rookie	§230	9 a.m.–3 p.m.	Junker	0	0	0	2	0	0	0	-3/0/-15/0/-45/-2/0
Science	Field Researcher	§320	9 a.m.–3 p.m.	Std. Car	0	0	0	0	2	0	0	-3/0/-5/0/-38/-4/0
Xtreme	Whitewater Guide	§325	9 a.m.–3 p.m.	SUV	0	0	0	2	0	0	1	-3/0/-10/0/-45/-4/0
Music	Wedding Singer	§250	9 a.m.–3 p.m.	Junker	0	0	0	0	0	2	0	0/0/0/0/-36/0/0
Slacker	Life Guard	§220	9 a.m.–3 p.m.	"Life Guard Jeep"	0	0	0	2	0	0	1	0/0/-6/0/-36/0/0
Paranormal	Tarot Card Reader	§110	5 p.m.–11 p.m.	Junker	0	0	1	0	0	2	0	0/0/0/0/-36/0/0
Journalism	Tabloid Writer	§155	9 a.m.–3 p.m.	Std. Car	0	0	0	0	0	2	1	0/0/0/0/-36/0/0
Hacker	Web Master	§175	6 p.m.–2 a.m.	Junker	0	2	0	0	0	0	0	0/0/0/0/-32/0/0

REQUIREMENTS FOR LEVEL 4 POSITIONS

CAREER TRACK	POSITION	DAILY PAY	HOURS	CAR POOL VEHICLE	COOKING	REPAIR	CHARISMA	BODY	LOGIC	CREATIVITY	FAMILY FRIENDS	DAILY MOTIVE DECAY (HUNGER/COMFORT/ HYGIENE/BLADDER/ ENERGY/FUN/SOCIAL)
Business	Junior Executive	§320	9 a.m.–4 p.m.	Std. Car	0	2	2	0	0	0	1	-7/0/-10/0/-42/-7/0
Entertainment	Stunt Double	§275	9 a.m.–4 p.m.	Std. Car	0	0	2	2	0	0	2	-7/0/-10/0/-42/-7/00
Law Enforcement	Desk Sergeant	§440	9 a.m.–3 p.m.	Squad Car	0	2	0	2	0	0	1	-7/0/-10/0/-42/-7/0
Life of Crime	Con Artist	§350	9 a.m.–3 p.m.	Std. Car	0	0	1	2	0	1	2	-7/0/-10/0/-42/-7/0
Medicine	Intern	§410	9 a.m.–6 p.m.	Std. Car	0	2	0	2	0	0	2	-7/0/-10/0/-42/-7/0
Military	Junior Officer	§450	9 a.m.–3 p.m.	Military Jeep	0	1	2	2	0	0	0	-7/0/-20/0/-42/-8/0
Politics	Campaign Manager	§430	9 a.m.–6 p.m.	Std. Car	0	0	2	0	1	0	2	-7/0/-10/0/-42/-7/0
Pro Athlete	Starter	§300	9 a.m.–3 p.m.	Std. Car	0	0	0	5	0	0	1	-7/0/-20/0/-50/-2/0
Science	Science Teacher	§375	9 a.m.–4 p.m.	Std. Car	0	0	1	0	3	0	1	-7/0/-10/0/-40/-7/0
Xtreme	Xtreme Circuit Pro	§400	9 a.m.–3 p.m.	SUV	0	1	0	4	0	0	2	-7/0/-20/0/-50/-2/0
Music	Lounge Singer	§250	9 p.m.–4 a.m.	Military Jeep	0	0	0	0	0	5	2	0/0/0/0/-40/0/0
Slacker	Record Store Clerk	§180	12 p.m.–5 p.m.	Junker	0	0	2	2	0	0	2	0/0/-5/0/-40/0/0
Paranormal	Hypnotist	§300	10 a.m.–4 p.m.	Junker	0	0	2	0	2	2	1	-6/0/-6/0/-42/0/0
Journalism	Paparazzi	§350	5 p.m.–1 a.m.	Staff Sedan	0	0	2	0	0	2	2	0/0/0/0/-40/0/0
Hacker	Hacker	§240	12 a.m.–9 a.m.	Junker	0	3	0	0	2	0	0	0/0/0/0/-36/0/0

REQUIREMENTS FOR LEVEL 5 POSITIONS

Career Track	Position	Daily Pay	Hours	Car Pool Vehicle	Cooking	Repair	Charisma	Body	Logic	Creativity	Family Friends	Daily Motive Decay (Hunger/Comfort/Hygiene/Bladder/Energy/Fun/Social)
Business	Executive	§400	9 a.m.–4 p.m.	Std. Car	0	2	2	0	2	0	3	-10/0/-15/0/-46/-10/0
Entertainment	B-Movie Star	§375	10 a.m.–5 p.m.	Std. Car	0	0	3	3	0	1	4	-10/0/-15/0/-46/-10/0
Law Enforcement	Vice Squad	§490	10 p.m.–4a.m.	Squad Car	0	3	0	4	0	0	2	-10/0/-15/0/-46/-10/0
Life of Crime	Getaway Driver	§425	5 p.m.–1a.m.	Std. Car	0	2	1	2	0	2	3	-10/0/-10/0/-46/-10/0
Medicine	Resident	§480	9 p.m.–4a.m.	Std. Car	0	3	0	2	2	0	3	-10/0/-15/0/-46/-10/0
Military	Counter-Intelligence	§500	9 a.m.–3 p.m.	Military Jeep	1	1	2	4	0	0	0	-10/0/-25/0/-46/-12/0
Politics	City Council Member	§485	9 a.m.–3 p.m.	Town Car	0	0	3	1	1	0	4	-10/0/-15/0/-46/-8/0
Pro Athlete	All-Star	§385	9 a.m.–3 p.m.	SUV	0	1	1	6	0	0	3	-10/0/-25/0/-55/-3/0
Science	Project Leader	§450	9 a.m.–5 p.m.	Std. Car	0	0	2	0	4	1	3	-10/0/-12/0/-43/-8/0
Xtreme	Bush Pilot	§475	9 a.m.–3 p.m.	SUV	1	2	0	4	1	0	3	-10/0/-15/0/-46/-5/-10
Music	High School Band Teacher	§325	7 a.m.–2 p.m.	Junker	0	2	0	0	0	6	2	-7/0/-7/0/-42/-7/0
Slacker	Party D. J.	§220	11 p.m.–4 a.m.	Junker	0	0	4	2	0	0	4	-5/0/-5/0/-40/0/0
Paranormal	Medium	§375	8 p.m.–2 a.m.	Junker	0	0	2	0	3	2	3	-6/0/-6/0/-42/-6/0
Journalism	Newspaper Reporter	§420	3 a.m.–10 a.m.	Staff Sedan	0	0	2	0	2	4	2	-7/0/-7/0/-42/0/0
Hacker Consultant	Security	§400	10 a.m.–7 p.m.	Std. Car	0	4	0	0	4	0	2	0/0/0/0/-36/0/0

REQUIREMENTS FOR LEVEL 6 POSITIONS

Career Track	Position	Daily Pay	Hours	Car Pool Vehicle	Cooking	Repair	Charisma	Body	Logic	Creativity	Family Friends	Daily Motive Decay (Hunger/Comfort/Hygiene/Bladder/Energy/Fun/Social)
Business	Senior Manager	§520	9 a.m.–4 p.m.	Std. Car	0	2	3	0	3	2	6	-14/0/-20/0/-50/-13/0
Entertainment	Supporting Player	§500	10 a.m.–6 p.m.	Limo	0	1	4	4	0	2	6	-14/0/-20/0/-50/-13/0
Law Enforcement	Detective	§540	9 a.m.–3 p.m.	Squad Car	1	3	1	5	1	0	4	-14/0/-20/0/-50/-13/0
Life of Crime	Bank Robber	§530	3 p.m.–11 p.m.	Town Car	0	3	2	3	1	2	4	-14/0/-15/0/-50/-13/-5
Medicine	GP	§550	10 a.m.–6 p.m.	Town Car	0	3	1	3	4	0	4	-14/0/-20/0/-50/-13/0
Military	Flight Officer	§550	9 a.m.–3 p.m.	Military Jeep	1	2	4	4	1	0	1	-14/0/-28/0/-50/-15/0
Politics	State Assembly-person	§540	9 a.m.–4 p.m.	Town Car	0	0	4	2	1	1	6	-14/0/-20/0/-50/-12/-3
Pro Athlete	MVP	§510	9 a.m.–3 p.m.	SUV	0	2	2	7	0	0	5	-14/0/-30/0/-60/-4/0
Science	Inventor	§540	10 a.m.–7 p.m.	Town Car	0	2	2	0	4	3	4	-14/0/-15/0/-45/-9/-8
Xtreme	Mountain Climber	§550	9 a.m.–3 p.m.	SUV	1	4	0	6	1	0	4	-14/0/-30/0/-60/0/0
Music	Roadie	§400	11 p.m.–8 p.m.	Junker	0	5	0	0	0	7	5	0/0/0/0/-45/0/0
Slacker	Projectionist	§280	6 p.m.–1 a.m.	Junker	0	3	4	2	0	0	6	0/0/0/0/-45/0/0
Paranormal	Douser	§480	6 a.m.–3 p.m.	Junker	0	0	3	1	4	2	5	-8/0/-16/0/-48/-8/0
Journalism	Meteorologist	§510	5 a.m.–1 p.m.	Staff Sedan	0	0	3	1	3	5	4	-8/0/-8/0/-48/0/0
Hacker	Game Designer	§610	2 p.m.–11 p.m.	Std. Car	0	4	0	0	4	4	3	-9/0/-9/0/-45/-9/0

REQUIREMENTS FOR LEVEL 7 POSITIONS

Career Track	Position	Daily Pay	Hours	Car Pool Vehicle	Cooking	Repair	Charisma	Body	Logic	Creativity	Family Friends	Daily Motive Decay (Hunger/Comfort/Hygiene/Bladder/Energy/Fun/Social)
Business	Vice President	§660	9 a.m.–5 p.m.	Town Car	0	2	4	2	4	2	8	-18/0/-25/0/-54/-16/0
Entertainment	TV Star	§650	10 a.m.–6 p.m.	Limo	0	1	6	5	0	3	8	-18/0/-25/0/-54/-16/0
Law Enforcement	Lieutenant	§590	9 a.m.–3 p.m.	Limo	1	3	2	5	3	1	6	-18/0/-25/0/-54/-16/0
Life of Crime	Cat Burglar	§640	9 p.m.–3a.m.	Town Car	1	3	2	5	2	3	6	-18/0/-20/0/-54/-16/0
Medicine	Specialist	§625	10 p.m.–4a.m.	Town Car	0	4	2	4	4	1	5	-18/0/-25/0/-54/-16/0
Military	Senior Officer	§580	9 a.m.–3 p.m.	Military Jeep	1	3	4	5	3	0	3	-18/0/-31/0/-55/-20/0
Politics	Congress-person	§600	9 a.m.–3 p.m.	Town Car	0	0	4	3	3	2	9	-18/0/-25/0/-54/-18/-7
Pro Athlete	Superstar	§680	9 a.m.–4 p.m.	SUV	1	2	3	8	0	0	7	-18/0/-35/0/-65/-5/0
Science	Scholar	§640	10 a.m.–3 p.m.	Town Car	0	4	2	0	6	4	5	-18/0/-20/0/-48/-10/-10
Xtreme	Photo-journalist	§650	9 a.m.–3 p.m.	SUV	1	5	2	6	1	3	5	-18/0/-25/0/-54/-16/0
Music	Back-up Musician	§550	12 p.m.–9 p.m.	Std. Car	0	5	0	4	0	8	8	-18/0/-18/0/-54/-9/0
Slacker	Video Editor	§350	12 p.m.–6 p.m.	Std. Car	0	5	4	2	0	0	7	-12/0/-24/0/-48/0/0
Paranormal	Police Psychic	§600	6 p.m.–2 a.m.	Squad Car	0	1	5	1	5	3	6	-16/0/-24/0/-48/-8/0
Journalism	TV Reporter	§660	12 p.m.–8 p.m.	Staff Sedan	0	0	6	2	3	5	6	-16/0/-24/0/-48/-16/-8
Hacker	Internet Entrepreneur	§800	10 a.m.–8 p.m.	SUV	0	4	2	0	5	6	5	-10/0/-20/0/-40/-10/0

REQUIREMENTS FOR LEVEL 8 POSITIONS

Career Track	Position	Daily Pay	Hours	Car Pool Vehicle	Cooking	Repair	Charisma	Body	Logic	Creativity	Family Friends	Daily Motive Decay (Hunger/Comfort/Hygiene/Bladder/Energy/Fun/Social)
Business	President	§800	9 a.m.–5 p.m.	Town Car	0	2	5	2	6	3	10	-22/0/-30/0/-58/-19/0
Entertainment	Feature Star	§900	5 p.m.–1a.m.	Limo	0	2	7	6	0	4	10	-22/0/-30/0/-58/-19/0
Law Enforcement	SWAT Team Leader	§625	9 a.m.–3 p.m.	Limo	1	4	3	6	5	1	8	-22/0/-30/0/-58/-19/0
Life of Crime	Counterfeiter	§760	9 p.m.–3a.m.	Town Car	1	5	2	5	3	5	8	-22/0/-25/0/-58/-19/-15
Medicine	Surgeon	§700	10 p.m.–4a.m.	Town Car	0	4	3	5	6	2	7	-22/0/-30/0/-58/-19/0
Military	Commander	§600	9 a.m.–3 p.m.	Military Jeep	1	6	5	5	5	0	5	-22/0/-33/0/-60/-25/0
Politics	Judge	§650	9 a.m.–3 p.m.	Town Car	0	0	5	4	4	3	11	-22/0/-30/0/-58/-22/-11
Pro Athlete	Assistant Coach	§850	9 a.m.–2 p.m.	SUV	2	2	4	9	0	1	9	-22/0/-40/0/-70/-6/0
Science	Top Secret Researcher	§740	10 a.m.–3 p.m.	Town Car	1	6	4	0	7	4	7	-22/0/-25/0/-52/-12/-13
Xtreme	Treasure Hunter	§725	10 a.m.–5 p.m.	SUV	1	6	3	7	3	4	7	-22/0/-34/0/-60/-15/-5
Music	Studio Musician	§700	11 a.m.–6 p.m.	SUV	0	5	2	5	0	10	9	-14/0/-21/0/-56/-14/0
Slacker	Freelance Photographer	§400	12 p.m.–5 p.m.	SUV	0	5	7	3	0	0	10	-20/0/-25/0/-45/0/0
Paranormal	UFO Investigator	§810	11 p.m.–6 a.m.	Squad Car	0	1	6	1	7	4	10	-21/0/-28/0/-56/-14/0
Journalism	Investigative Reporter	§850	10 a.m.–5 p.m.	SUV	0	0	8	2	4	5	9	-14/0/-21/0/-49/-14/-2
Hacker	Software CEO	§1,100	10 a.m.–7 p.m.	Town Car	0	4	4	0	7	7	6	-9/0/-18/0/-54/-9/0

REQUIREMENTS FOR LEVEL 9 POSITIONS

Career Track	Position	Daily Pay	Hours	Car Pool Vehicle	Cooking	Repair	Charisma	Body	Logic	Creativity	Family Friends	Daily Motive Decay (Hunger/Comfort/Hygiene/Bladder/Energy/Fun/Social)
Business	CEO	§950	9 a.m.–4 p.m.	Limo	0	2	6	2	7	5	12	-26/0/-35/0/-62/-22/0
Entertainment	Broadway Star	§1,100	10 a.m.–5 p.m.	Limo	0	2	8	7	0	7	12	-26/0/-35/0/-62/-22/0
Law Enforcement	Police Chief	§650	9 a.m.–5 p.m.	Limo	1	4	4	7	7	3	10	-26/0/-35/0/-62/-22/0
Life of Crime	Smuggler	§900	9 a.m.–3 p.m.	Town Car	1	5	5	6	3	6	10	-26/0/-30/0/-62/-22/-20
Medicine	Medical Researcher	§775	9 p.m.–4a.m.	Limo	0	5	4	6	8	3	9	-26/0/-35/0/-62/-22/0
Military	Astronaut	§625	9 a.m.–3 p.m.	Limo	1	9	5	8	6	0	6	-26/0/-35/0/-65/-30/0
Politics	Senator	§700	9 a.m.–6 p.m.	Limo	0	0	6	5	6	4	14	-26/0/-35/0/-62/-26/-15
Pro Athlete	Coach	§1,000	9 a.m.–3 p.m.	SUV	3	2	6	10	0	2	11	-26/0/-45/0/-75/-8/0
Science	Theorist	§870	10 a.m.–2 p.m.	Town Car	1	7	4	0	9	7	8	-26/0/-30/0/-56/-16/-16
Xtreme	Grand Prix Driver	§825	10 a.m.–4 p.m.	Bentley	1	6	5	7	5	7	9	-26/0/-35/0/-62/-5/-10
Music	Rock Star	§110	5 p.m.–2 a.m.	Limo	0	5	7	7	0	10	12	-18/0/-27/0/-54/-18/0
Slacker	Personal Tour Guide	§450	2 p.m.–7 p.m.	SUV	0	5	8	6	0	0	12	-20/0/-30/0/-45/0/0
Paranormal	Exorcist	§1,000	10 a.m.–3 p.m.	Bentley	0	1	8	1	7	5	13	-20/0/-30/0/-55/-20/-5
Journalism	National News Anchor	§975	11 a.m.–8 p.m.	Limo	0	0	9	5	5	6	11	-18/0/-27/0/-54/-18/-9
Hacker	Venture Capitalist	§1,300	11 a.m.–8 p.m.	Bentley	0	5	6	0	8	9	8	-27/0/-36/0/-63/-18/0

REQUIREMENTS FOR LEVEL 10 POSITIONS

Career Track	Position	Daily Pay	Hours	Car Pool Vehicle	Cooking	Repair	Charisma	Body	Logic	Creativity	Family Friends	Daily Motive Decay (Hunger/Comfort/Hygiene/Bladder/Energy/Fun/Social)
Business	Business Tycoon	§1,200	9 a.m.–3 p.m.	Limo	0	2	8	2	9	6	14	-30/0/-40/0/-66/-25/0
Entertainment	Superstar	§1,400	10 a.m.–3 p.m.	Limo	0	2	10	8	0	10	14	-30/0/-40/0/-66/-25/0
Law Enforcement	Captain Hero	§700	10 a.m.–4 p.m.	Limo	1	4	6	7	10	5	12	-20/-80/-45/-25/-60/0/0
Life of Crime	Criminal Mastermind	§1,100	6 p.m.–12a.m.	Limo	2	5	7	6	4	8	12	-30/0/-35/0/-66/-25/-25
Medicine	Chief of Hospital Staff	§850	9 p.m.–4a.m.	Limo	0	6	6	7	9	4	11	-30/0/-40/0/-66/-25/0
Military	General	§650	9 a.m.–3 p.m.	Staff Sedan	1	10	7	10	9	0	8	-30/0/-40/0/-70/-35/0
Politics	Mayor	§750	9 a.m.–3 p.m.	Limo	0	0	9	5	7	5	17	-30/0/-40/0/-66/-30/-20
Pro Athlete	Hall of Famer	§1,300	9 a.m.–3 p.m.	Limo	4	2	9	10	0	3	13	-30/0/-50/0/-80/-10/0
Science	Mad Scientist	§1,000	10 a.m.–2 p.m.	Limo	2	8	5	0	10	10	10	-30/0/-35/0/-60/-20/-20
Xtreme	International Spy	§925	11 a.m.–5 p.m.	Bentley	2	6	8	8	6	9	11	-30/0/-30/0/-70/-20/-15
Music	Celebrity Activist	§1,400	10 a.m.–3 p.m.	Limo	0	5	10	7	4	10	15	-30/0/-40/0/-65/-25/+5
Slacker	Professional Party Guest	§600	10 p.m.–2 a.m.	Limo	0	5	10	9	0	0	15	-28/0/-40/0/-44/0/0
Paranormal	Cult Leader	§1,200	10 a.m.–4 p.m.	Limo	0	2	10	2	9	7	17	-24/0/-30/0/-60/-18/+12
Journalism	Talk Show Host	§1,200	1 p.m.–5 p.m.	Limo	0	0	10	5	7	7	14	-28/0/-36/0/-64/-24/+12
Hacker	Information Overlord	§1,550	11 a.m.–8 p.m.	Limo	0	7	8	0	10	10	8	-27/0/-36/0/-63/-18/0

School

Sim kids don't have careers, of course. But they do have to go to school and keep their grades up. Lazy students face expulsion from the family (and the game) by being sent to Military School. Here's the lowdown on academics in *The Sims*.

Going to School

The school bus arrives daily at 8 a.m. outside households that include Sim kids. Kids with mood ratings in the green go to the bus automatically unless you direct them to another activity. A Sim kid who goes to a bus that's been waiting more than 45 minutes runs to it automatically.

Fig. 6-9. Send your kids to the school bus in a good mood to boost Report Card grades each day.

The Report Card

Click on the Job button on the Control Panel to view your Sim kid's current Report Card, which displays a single grade. This grade improves a level—from B+ to A–, for example—every day the kid rides the bus to school in a good mood. Naturally, the reverse is true, as well. The Report Card grade drops a level every day the kid leaves in a bad mood.

Fig. 6-10. Keep an eye on that Report Card grade. If it drops to a D or below, try boosting it with some home study.

Kids who maintain an A+ Report Card randomly get small cash awards, accompanied by dialog such as, "Beth just won the spelling bee at school. Grandma sends her §100."

Studying for School

Each kid starts out with a B grade. Children with grades lower than A+ are given the pie-menu choice to Study for School when you click on a bookshelf. Kids don't *have* to study at home if they continue to attend school in a good mood. But it's one way to speed up grade inflation.

The *Livin' Large* expansion pack adds another object kids can use to raise grades. The Horrorwitz "Star-Track" Backyard Telescope is fun to use (if you avoid alien abductions) and gives kids an academic boost at the same time. Adults can increase their Logic skill while gazing at the stars as well. At §2,100, though, the Horrorwitz is not cheap. Note also that the telescope can be placed and used outside only.

Kids with poor grades needn't study as long as higher-grade students to raise their grades. An F student need study only 20 minutes to get to a D–, 30 minutes to go from D– to D, 40 minutes from D to D+, and so on. This way, you can home-school your kids if you want, but doing so requires far more effort than if they rode the bus daily to school.

Of course, Sim kids won't study autonomously; you must direct them to. (*The Sims* is based on real life, after all.) Worse, kids won't study if they're in a bad mood. Overall, unhappy kids are unsuccessful kids.

Playing Hooky and Military School

Sim kids go to school autonomously in the morning if they're in a good mood. If they don't, you must encourage them to catch the morning bus. Every day a kid cuts classes, that kid's Report Card drops an entire letter grade—for example, from B– to C–. When the grade drops to D or below, a dialog box threatens your kid with Military School.

Fig. 6-11. Don't let your kid's Report Card drop to an F. Otherwise, you'll watch your little cadet march off to Military School—and out of the game.

If the Report Card is already at D or below when the bus arrives in the morning, you'll hear warning music and view a flashing Report Card. Last chance! Finally, if the grade drops to F, it's off to Military School with the little delinquent, who leaves the family forever—and nails your household with a §1,000 one-time charge for tuition. Ouch!

7
Sim Economics
101

Today's lecture covers the inexorable flow of simoleans, goods, services, and other sundry elements that make up *The Sims'* economic system. In particular, we explore how Sim objects depreciate (and, in some cases, appreciate) in worth, and explain how the SimCity Savings & Loan calculates those pesky bills you get in the mail every three days.

After that, we discuss the various services available to your Sim household. Finally, let us together stroll some of the darker side streets of Sim life—fire, theft, accident—and learn how to avoid or minimize losses from such disasters.

Fig. 7-1. The Holy Simolean. End-all, be-all? Or just another grand illusion? Fortunately, there's no room for philosophical musing in a strategy guide.

> **NOTE**
>
> Check out "Cheats & Quick Start Tips" to learn ways (some delightfully underhanded) to build money quickly in the early phases of your neighborhood.

Tips from the Testers

The hardest part of *The Sims* is starting a fresh family and advancing its members. Once you've established Family A (we'll call them the Waltons) with good jobs and a solid net worth, consider marrying or moving high-income Waltons into a Family B (the Newbies) that's just starting out.

The Walton family member's high wages can help stabilize the Newbies quickly, freeing up Newbies to build skills and make friends for their own advancement. It may seem kind of mercenary, but you can always marry the Walton member back into his or her original family later.

—Andrew Blomquist, Tester

Net Worth

With the exception of the Goths and the Newbies, all families start with a net worth of 20,000 simoleans. Net worth includes lot price, the depreciated value of the house (and other architectural items), the depreciated value of objects, and household funds. Lots come in three sizes; size and location determine lot cost. When a family moves, all purchased objects are deleted from the house and the depreciated value is credited to the family's funds.

Fig. 7-2. Every new family starts with 20,000 simoleans. The bigger the family, the more money you should allocate to house size and multiple bathrooms. (Crowded bathrooms block the flow of happiness in ANY home.)

Object Depreciation

Object depreciation is relevant to your Sim family's net worth and bill amounts, and to the amount of money you get when you sell objects. Each object you purchase (other than art objects, which follow different rules) has an initial and daily depreciation, as well as a depreciation limit.

Initial Depreciation

You may return the stuff you buy for a full refund before midnight on the day of your purchase. After your Sims own an item for one full Sim day, however, its worth decreases by an initial depreciation value—a percentage of the object's original cost. This percentage varies according to the object's category when sorted by function in the catalog—Electronics, Decorative, Lighting, and so forth.

The Object Depreciation table at the end of this section provides a complete list of items and their initial depreciation.

Daily Depreciation

Again, the initial depreciation lowers an item's value after midnight on the day of purchase. After that, the item continues to depreciate at a fixed amount every Sim day until it reaches a limit. (See the following "Depreciation Limit" section.) This daily depreciation is 1 percent of the item's original value.

The Object Depreciation table later in this section provides a complete list of items and their daily depreciation.

Depreciation Limit

Every item's value decreases by an initial depreciation after midnight on the day of purchase, and

Fig. 7-3. Most items you can purchase in THE SIMS depreciate. This Exerto exercise machine originally cost §700, but it's depreciated §140 over time.

then drops daily to a given limit. Once it reaches this value, it remains there for the rest of its stay in your household. The Object Depreciation table provides a complete list of items and their depreciation limits.

Value of Broken Items

Oops! I dropped it. Too bad. If you sell a broken object, you get only half its current depreciated value. Hey, what did you expect?

Art Appreciation/Depreciation

Paintings and sculptures appreciate and depreciate randomly every day. In general, the trend is upward. Beyond that, all we can say is it's up to the whims of the snooty Sim art crowd.

TIP

The garden gnomes you build with the KraftKing Woodworking Table appreciate in value. The better your Mechanical skill, the more they're worth.

OBJECT DEPRECIATION

PURCHASE PRICE	NAME	INITIAL DEPRECIATION	DAILY DEPRECIATION	DEPRECIATION LIMIT
§50	Alarm: Smoke	§12	§0	§10
§250	Alarm: Burglar	§62	§2	§50
§200	Aquarium	§30	§2	§80
§800	Bar	§120	§8	§320
§780	Bar (Beach Boss)	§117	§8	§312
§350	Barbecue	§70	§4	§105
§650	Basketball Hoop	§98	§6	§260
§450	Bed: Double (Cheap Eaze)	§68	§4	§180
§1,000	Bed: Double (Napoleon)	§150	§10	§400
§3,000	Bed: Double (Mission)	§450	§30	§1,200
§3,650	Bed: Double (Four-Poster)	§547	§36	§1,460
§4,500	Bed: Double (Vibromatic)	§675	§45	§1,800
§300	Bed: Single (Spartan)	§45	§3	§120
§450	Bed: Single (Tyke Nyte)	§68	§4	§180
§250	Bench: Garden	§38	§2	§100
§2,000	Bench: Gothic Revival	§300	§20	§400
§250	Bookshelf: Pine	§38	§2	§100
§500	Bookshelf: Amishim	§75	§5	§200
§900	Bookshelf: Libri di Regina	§135	§9	§360
§910	Bookshelf: The Swing	§136	§9	§364
§150	Chair: Deck	§22	§2	§60
§80	Chair: Dining (Werkbunnst)	§12	§1	§32
§200	Chair: Dining (Teak)	§30	§2	§80
§210	Chair: Dining (Sir Laxalot)	§31	§2	§84
§299	Chair: Dining (The "M")	§45	§3	§119
§1,200	Chair: Dining (El Tomayo)	§180	§12	§480

OBJECT DEPRECIATION, continued

PURCHASE PRICE	NAME	INITIAL DEPRECIATION	DAILY DEPRECIATION	DEPRECIATION LIMIT
§600	Chair: Dining (Empress)	§90	§6	§240
§1,200	Chair: Dining (Parisienne)	§180	§12	§480
§80	Chair: Living Room (Wicker)	§12	§1	§32
§155	Chair: Living Room (Satinistics)	§23	§2	§62
§250	Chair: Living Room (Country Class)	§38	§2	§100
§335	Chair: Living Room (Etherette)	§50	§3	§134
§450	Chair: Living Room (Citronel)	§68	§4	§180
§460	Chair: Living Room (Frogg)	§460	§5	§184
§500	Chair: Living Room (Sarrbach)	§75	§5	§200
§840	Chair: Living Room (Egg)	§126	§8	§336
§1,200	Chair: Living Room (Ebonized Victorian)	§180	§12	§480
§1,200	Chair: Living Room (Manchester)	§180	§12	§480
§1,440	Chair: Living Room (Duke of Earle)	§216	§14	§576
§100	Chair: Office	§15	§1	§40
§250	Chair: Recliner (Back Slack)	§38	§2	§100
§850	Chair: Recliner (Von Braun)	§128	§8	§340
§980	Chemistry Lab	§147	§10	§392
§500	Chess Set	§75	§5	§200
§199	Christmas Tree	§30	§2	§80
§30	Clock: Alarm	§4	§0	§12
§180	Clock: Cuckoo	§27	§2	§72
§3,500	Clock: Grandfather	§525	§35	§1,400
§450	Coffee: Espresso Machine	§90	§4	§135
§85	Coffeemaker	§17	§1	§26
§999	Computer (Moneywell)	§250	§10	§200
§1,800	Computer (Microscotch)	§450	§18	§360
§2,800	Computer (Brahma 2000)	§700	§28	§560
§6,500	Computer (Marco)	§1,625	§65	§1,300
§400	Counter: Bath (Count Blanc)	§60	§4	§160
§150	Counter: Kitchen (NuMica)	§22	§2	§60
§250	Counter: Kitchen (Tiled)	§38	§2	§100
§425	Counter: Kitchen (Cornerstone)	§64	§4	§170
§800	Counter: Kitchen (Barcelona: Out)	§120	§8	§320
§800	Counter: Kitchen (Barcelona: In)	§120	§8	§320
§760	Crystal Ball	§114	§8	§304
§80	Desk (Mesquite)	§12	§1	§32

Purchase Price	Name	Initial Depreciation	Daily Depreciation	Depreciation Limit
§220	Desk (Cupertino)	§33	§2	§88
§800	Desk (Redmond)	§120	§8	§320
§999	Desk (O'Mann)	§150	§10	§400
§550	Dishwasher (Dish Duster)	§110	§6	§165
§950	Dishwasher (Fuzzy Logic)	§190	§10	§285
§180	Dollhouse	§27	§2	§72
§250	Dresser (Pinegulcher)	§38	§2	§100
§300	Dresser (Kinderstuff)	§45	§3	§120
§510	Dresser (Makutu)	§76	§5	§204
§980	Dresser (Guido)	§84	§10	§224
§550	Dresser (Oak Armoire)	§82	§6	§220
§1,200	Dresser (Antique Armoire)	§180	§12	§480
§2,500	Dresser (Fantzi)	§375	§25	§1,000
§250	Easel	§38	§2	§100
§700	Exercise Machine	§105	§7	§280
§12	Flamingo	§2	§0	§5
§220	Food Processor	§44	§2	§66
§700	Fountain	§105	§7	§280
§600	Fridge (Llamark)	§120	§6	§180
§1,200	Fridge (Porcina)	§240	§12	§360
§2,500	Fridge (Freeze Secret)	§500	§25	§750
§2,750	Fridge (Olde Thyme)	§550	§27	§825
§120	Guinea Pig	§18	§1	§48
§580	Guitar	§87	§6	§232
§6,500	Hot Tub	§1,300	§65	§1,950
§1,199	Jukebox	§180	§11	§231
§375	Lamp: Antique	§56	§4	§150
§50	Lamp: Floor (Halogen)	§8	§0	§20
§70	Lamp: Floor (Tiki Torch)	§10	§1	§28
§100	Lamp: Floor (Lumpen)	§15	§1	§40
§130	Lamp: Floor (Cupidity)	§19	§1	§52
§160	Lamp: Floor (Gam Sarfatti)	§24	§2	§64
§170	Lamp: Floor (Blue Note)	§25	§2	§68
§180	Lamp: Floor (Mica Tube)	§27	§2	§72
§250	Lamp: Floor (Biomushric)	§37	§2	§100
§250	Lamp: Floor (Methanopolis)	§37	§2	§100
§300	Lamp: Floor (Cone Head)	§45	§3	§120

OBJECT DEPRECIATION, continued

PURCHASE PRICE	NAME	INITIAL DEPRECIATION	DAILY DEPRECIATION	DEPRECIATION LIMIT
§330	Lamp: Floor (Torchemada)	§49	§3	§132
§350	Lamp: Floor (Torchosteronne)	§52	§4	§140
§50	Lamp: Garden	§7	§1	§20
§125	Lamp: Garden (Greek Fire)	§20	§1	§50
§1,250	Lamp: Garden (Medieval)	§187	§12	§500
§35	Lamp: Sconce (White Globe)	§5	§0	§14
§85	Lamp: Sconce (Oval Glass)	§13	§1	§34
§110	Lamp: Sconce (Top Brass)	§16	§1	§44
§110	Lamp: Sconce (Torchemada)	§16	§1	§44
§135	Lamp: Sconce (Blue Plate)	§20	§1	§54
§295	Lamp: Sconce (NeoRococo)	§44	§3	§118
§360	Lamp: Sconce (Sisters of Mercy)	§54	§4	§144
§1,150	Lamp: Sconce (Alcove Knight)	§172	§11	§460
§25	Lamp: Table (Bottle)	§4	§0	§10
§85	Lamp: Table (Ceramiche)	§13	§1	§34
§120	Lamp: Table (Femme De Luxe)	§18	§1	§48
§180	Lamp: Table (Elite)	§27	§2	§72
§200	Lamp: Table (Torchosteronne)	§30	§2	§80
§300	Lamp: Table (Antique)	§45	§3	§120
§80	Lamp: Love 'n Haight	§12	§1	§32
§125	Medicine Cabinet	§19	§1	§50
§175	Menorah	§26	§2	§70
§250	Microwave	§50	§2	§75
§150	Mirror: Floor	§22	§2	§60
§100	Mirror: Wall	§15	§1	§40
§1,100	Mirror: Wall (Optilopticon)	§165	§11	§440
§50	Phone: Tabletop	§12	§0	§10
§75	Phone: Wall	§19	§1	§15
§3,500	Piano	§525	§35	§1,400
§5,399	Piano (Liebefunkenmann)	§810	§54	§2,160
§1,800	Pinball Machine	§450	§18	§360
§90	Plant: Big (Potted Palm)	§13	§1	§36
§120	Plant: Big (Rubber)	§18	§1	§48
§150	Plant: Big (Cactus)	§22	§2	§60
§160	Plant: Big (Jade)	§24	§2	§64
§170	Plant: Big (Bird of Paradise)	§25	§2	§68

Purchase Price	Name	Initial Depreciation	Daily Depreciation	Depreciation Limit
§30	Plant: Small (Violets)	§4	§0	§12
§35	Plant: Small (Spider)	§5	§0	§14
§45	Plant: Small (Geranium)	§7	§0	§18
§1,200	Play Structure	§180	§12	§480
§4,200	Pool Table	§630	§42	§1,680
§15,000	Robot: Servo	§3,750	§150	§6,000
§650	Shower	§130	§6	§195
§400	Sink: Bathroom Pedestal	§80	§4	§120
§250	Sink: Kitchen (Single)	§50	§2	§75
§500	Sink: Kitchen (Double)	§100	§5	§150
§600	Sink: Stone	§120	§6	§180
§1,750	Slot Machine	§437	§17	§700
§150	Sofa: Loveseat (Contempo)	§22	§2	§60
§160	Sofa: Loveseat (Indoor-Outdoor)	§24	§2	§64
§240	Sofa: Loveseat (Satinistics)	§36	§2	§96
§340	Sofa: Loveseat (Country)	§51	§3	§136
§360	Sofa: Loveseat (Blue Pinstripe)	§54	§4	§144
§875	Sofa: Loveseat (Luxuriare)	§131	§9	§350
§1,445	Sofa: Loveseat (Le Grande Guignol)	§217	§14	§578
§180	Sofa (Recycled)	§27	§2	§72
§200	Sofa (Contempo)	§30	§2	§80
§220	Sofa (SimSafari)	§33	§2	§88
§400	Sofa (Blue Pinstripe)	§60	§4	§160
§450	Sofa (Country)	§68	§4	§180
§575	Sofa (Sofasaurus)	§86	§6	§230
§1,100	Sofa (Deiter)	§165	§11	§440
§1,450	Sofa (Dolce)	§218	§14	§580
§1,600	Sofa (Red Matter)	§240	§16	§640
§100	Stereo: Boom Box	§25	§1	§20
§650	Stereo (Zimantz)	§162	§6	§130
§2,550	Stereo (Strings)	§638	§26	§510
§400	Stove (Dialectric)	§80	§4	§120
§1,000	Stove (Pyrotorre)	§200	§10	§300
§1,100	Stove (CiaoTime)	§220	§11	§330
§1,600	Stove (Old Thyme)	§320	§16	§480
§95	Table: Dining (NuMica)	§14	§1	§38
200	Table: Dining (Colonial)	§30	§2	§80

OBJECT DEPRECIATION, continued

Purchase Price	Name	Initial Depreciation	Daily Depreciation	Depreciation Limit
§450	Table: Dining (Mesa)	§68	§4	§180
§450	Table: Dining (Retratech)	§67	§4	§180
§850	Table: Dining (The "M")	§127	§8	§340
§1,200	Table: Dining (Parisienne)	§180	§12	§480
§1,500	Table: Dining (El Tomayo)	§225	§15	§600
§40	Table: End (Pinegulcher)	§6	§0	§16
§55	Table: End (Wicker)	§8	§1	§22
§75	Table: End (KinderStuff)	§11	§1	§30
§79	Table: End (Rampa Lopside)	§12	§1	§32
§120	Table: End (Anywhere)	§18	§1	§48
§135	Table: End (Imperious)	§20	§1	§54
§250	Table: End (Mission)	§38	§2	§100
§300	Table: End (Sumpto)	§45	§3	§120
§399	Table: End (Queen's Rose)	§60	§4	§160
§200	Table: Outdoor (Backwoods)	§30	§2	§80
§2,100	Telescope	§315	§21	§840
§100	Toaster Oven	§20	§1	§30
§300	Toilet (Hygeia-O-Matic)	§60	§3	§90
§350	Toilet (Outhouse)	§70	§3	§105
§1,200	Toilet (Flush Force)	§240	§12	§360
§5	Tombstone/Urn	§1	§0	§2
§50	Toy Box	§8	§0	§20
§90	Toy Rocket	§13	§1	§36
§80	Train Set: Small	§20	§1	§16
§955	Train Set: Large	§239	§10	§191
§45	Trash Barrel	§7	§1	§18
§375	Trash Compactor	§75	§4	§112
§800	Tub (Justa)	§160	§8	§240
§1,500	Tub (Sani-Queen)	§300	§15	§450
§2,000	Tub (Antique)	§400	§20	§600
§3,200	Tub (Hydrothera)	§640	§32	§960
§85	TV (Monochrome)	§21	§1	§17
§500	TV (Trottco)	§125	§5	§100
§3,500	TV (Soma)	§875	§35	§700
§65	Voodoo Doll	§10	§1	§26
§2,300	VR Glasses	§575	§23	§460
§720	Woodworking Table	§108	§7	§288

A Note About Clothes

In *The Sims*, all clothes are free–normal clothes, work clothes, formal wear, swimwear, PJs. Isn't that nice? Not only that, but you can change your Sim's daily outfit at no charge. Well, not exactly no charge; you need a dresser or armoire. If you have one, click on it and select Change Clothes. Your Sim will don a different outfit from the one you assigned originally back in the Create a Sim screen. Selecting Change Clothes creates a new default outfit. That is, whenever your Sim takes a shower or bath or gets out of bed, he or she puts on this new set of clothes. Your Sim can also change their body type at the dresser/armoire—losing or gaining 100 pounds!

Build Depreciation

During any Build mode session, you can undo any action you've taken during that session for a full refund. Key words—*during that session!* Click the Undo button to undo the previous action and get a full refund. Click again to undo the *previous* previous action (going back in time), and get another full refund. You can click Undo as many times as you want to undo actions back to the beginning of the current session.

Fig. 7-4. Using the Undo button is the only way to get a full refund when taking back Build mode moves. If you delete or sell back (instead of Undo) this Chester Brick Column, for example, you lose 20 percent of the §100 you paid originally.

Once you leave Build mode, however, you can't return later and undo actions. You can sell most architecture items from previous Build mode sessions, but only for a depreciated value that remains constant no matter how old the item grows.

Also note that in Build mode, using the Undo button is the *only* way to get a full refund. Any other means of deletion, even during the current session, results in the set depreciation. For example, if you place a Chester Brick Column on your lot for §100, and then change your mind, the only way to get a full refund is to click Undo. If you use the Hand Tool to sell the Chester Brick Column or delete it, you'll receive only the column's depreciated value.

Build Items that Depreciate

You can undo the following Build items/actions for a full refund during the current Build mode session. After that, you may sell (or delete) them at a 20 percent depreciation rate (that is, you get back 80 percent of the original purchase price).

Important: Remember that covering over old wall or floor tiles eliminates any refund for them. You must remove (sell or delete) the old wall/floor coverings first in order to get money back.

- Walls
- Wallpaper (if deleted, but not if wallpapered over)
- Floor covering (if deleted, but not if covered over)
- Windows
- Doors
- Pool tiles, ladder, diving board
- Fireplaces
- Stairs

Fig. 7-5. Remember to delete old wall or floor coverings before you place new ones. If you just paper over old wallpaper, you recover NONE of the cost of the original materials.

Build Items You Can't Sell

You may undo the following build items/actions for a full refund during the current Build mode session, but you may not sell them at any time. If you delete them (select them with the Hand Tool and press (Delete)), you receive no money for them.

- Trees
- Flowers
- Shrubs
- Terrain changes

Bills and the Repo Man

Bills. We all have them. Rich or poor, you can't ignore bills—not in real life, and not in *The Sims*. So don't forget to check the mailbox. The letter carrier delivers bills to your Sims' home every three days. (The red mailbox flag goes up to alert you when bills arrive.) It takes 10 days for bills to become overdue. They turn yellow after three days, orange after six, and red after nine. Pay your bills by the 10th day, or the pitiless Repo Man will pay you a visit.

TIP

The Antique Lamp's genie can grant a "Money" spell that delivers either a pot of gold—or three sets of unpaid bills.

NOTE

The mailbox interaction Get Mail advertises with a high attenuation drop-off. That is, Sims must be near the mailbox to "hear" its ad and pick up their mail on their own. So workers returning in car pool at end of the day are likely to get their mail, but those watching TV in the house won't hear the mailbox "calling" to them.

Bill Calculation

In general, the more items you own, the more you owe. To determine what you owe, the happy accountants at SimCity Savings & Loan calculate 3 percent of the depreciated value of all your billable objects.

And what are billable objects? You *would* ask that question. Billable objects are everything you purchased (including Build mode materials) except columns, doors, paintings, dead plants, sculptures, shrubs, staircases, trees, and windows. Other rather obvious examples of non-billable objects are ash and trash piles, babies, bills, fires, floods, food, the mailbox, newspapers, and the outdoor trash can. Note that your bills are 10 percent less for each kid in the family, thanks to the dependent tax credit.

Repossession

Overdue bills. Everyone has them. By the dozens. Or wait, maybe that's just us. In any case, bills not paid by the 10th day after receipt prompt a visit from the green-clad Repo Man. The moment he arrives on the scene, both Buy and Build modes are disabled, so you can't quickly hock items and pay the bills: it's too late, man. There's nothing you can do.

Fig. 7-6. The Repo Man. You don't want to see this guy. Here he is, sucking up your very bed. Pay your bills within 10 days of receipt to avoid his costly visits

The Repo Man sucks the most valuable object in the house into his Fantastic Asimov 2000 miniaturization gun to cover the bill amount. If necessary, he'll take multiple objects to equal the value of the bill—starting with the most expensive.

Tips from the Testers

Here's an amusing way to avoid paying bills. If your Sim is using an object as the Repo Man repossesses it, you get the money back for the object as if you'd sold it. It requires some vigilance, though. Just keep track of what you owe. (Click on the bill pile to see the amount, but don't pay the bills.)

Immediately after a bill explodes (signifying its overdue status), switch to Buy mode and click the Hand Tool on every object. Find the object with the value closest to (but more than) your bills. Then, use that object over and over as the Repo Man arrives and repossesses it. Note: The Repo Man usually stands still at first and waits for you to finish. Just use the object again; he'll come grab it, and you'll get your refund.

—Andrew Blomquist, Maxis Tester

Services

Sim families have an extremely efficient network of services available to them. Firefighter, Police Officer, Maid, Repairman, Gardener, Newspaper and Pizza Deliverers—all are quite competent in *The Sims*. We highly recommend you take advantage of these services, regardless of your means.

Each service has a daily work-hour limit. Service providers work until they finish the job, unless the time exceeds the work-hour limit. When they finish their work, they flash the day's charge over their heads and leave. That amount is deducted from your household account automatically.

> **NOTE**
> The *Livin' Large* expansion pack offers you a nifty but very expensive replacement for the Maid, Repair, and Gardening services. Introducing Servo, the amazing robot who cooks, cleans, entertains and gives you backrubs when your Social is low, repairs, and gardens—all for a mere §15,000.

Not Enough Funds

If you don't have enough money in your account to pay a day's service fee, the service provider calls you a deadbeat (which, let's face it, you are) and procures household objects until their combined value equals the fee. This is only the case for the gardner, maid, and repairman. Like the Repo Man, service providers use the objects' current depreciated value, not the purchase price, and they start with objects they have already fixed.

> **NOTE**
> If a house goes back on the market (that is, you evict a family or everyone in the household dies), all hired services are discontinued. If you want services for a new family, you must hire them again.

Fig. 7-7. Extra! Extra! Get your SIM NEWS, delivered daily to your front walk.

Newspaper Delivery

The *Sim News* arrives automatically, delivered daily near the mailbox between 8:45 and 9 a.m. by your spunky paper-kid (at no charge at that!). Every midnight, that day's paper turns to trash. If five newspapers pile up in the front lawn, delivery is suspended until you "recycle" (toss out) at least one of the old papers.

Sims can use or read the newspaper as many times as they want before it turns to trash at midnight. But the paper features only one job offer per day. The same job offer will appear again and again if you keep looking there for a job on the same day.

Pizza Delivery

Pizza delivery is a 24-hour service. At §40 a pop, it's kind of pricey. When Freddy the Pizza Dude arrives, he won't hand over the pie if you can't pay. If you have sufficient funds, Freddy waits at the door until your Sim greets him and takes the pizza box. If no one answers the door within an hour, he'll leave.

> **Freddy the Pizza Dude:**
>
> Dude! Like I made it all the way from SimCity to your house in less than an hour!
>
> OK

Fig. 7-8. Freddy can deliver a §40 pizza in under an hour.

Fig. 7-9. Watering your own flowers can take a LOT of time out of your day. The Gardener keeps your flowers alive for a mere §10 an hour, and she waters in half the time a Sim takes.

Gardener

When hired, your friendly gardening service sends a highly qualified Gardener every three days. Work hours: 9 a.m. to 6 p.m. Your Gardener waters all flowers, inside and out, and stays as long as necessary (until quitting time) to finish the work. Hourly Rate: §10. Two interactions are possible with the Gardener: "Dismiss" means you send the Gardener home for the day; "Fire" means you discontinue the gardening service.

Maid

When you hire a Maid, she works every day. This woman not only looks good, she's a cleaning dynamo. The Maid makes unmade beds, washes dirty plates, picks up and takes out trash, and cleans anything that can be cleaned—sinks, tubs, showers, toilets, mops up floor puddles, you name it. Hourly Rate: §10. Work hours: 10 a.m. to 5 p.m. And she stays as long as it takes (until quitting time) to finish the work.

Two interactions are possible with the Maid: "Dismiss" means you send her home for the day; "Fire" means you discontinue the cleaning service.

Fig. 7-10. Maids are worth every penny they charge. Their thorough work lets you pile more personality points on fun, friendly traits like Outgoing and Nice.

Tips from the Testers

Sims don't need to be neat as long as they have a Maid, and for just §10 an hour, she's a major bargain. Even with a house full of disgusting slobs, the most she can cost you is §70 a day. Try this: When creating a new family, don't give any points to the Neat personality trait. Just hire a maid on Day One and forget about cleaning up.

—Andrew Blomquist, Tester

Repairman

When you call for repair help, your local service sends the Amazing Mr. Fixit. This guy repairs anything—TV, dishwasher, sink, shower, espresso machine, computer, pinball machine— *any* object that can break. In fact, if you have zero Mechanical skill and a broken TV, you have no choice but to call the repair man—it's the only way to fix it. He'll even unclog toilets and replace light bulbs. Hourly rate: §50—kind of steep, but with his super-high Mechanical skill, he rarely needs to stay more than an hour. If you're suddenly running low on funds, you can "Dismiss" the Repairman before he finishes his work.

Fig. 7-11. The Repairman works fast, saving you lots of time. His computer repair skills are impeccable, but he takes awhile (costing §100 or more).

TIP

Monsters spawned by drinking the pink potion brewed with the "Concatenation Station" Home Chemistry Lab can paint paintings that may be worth quite a few simoleons. Unfortunately, monsters also break stuff that can cost a few simoleans (or a lot of your time) to repair.

Tips from the Testers

If time is short and you have low Mechanical skill, use the Repairman. He's not outrageously expensive—compared to the costly wasted time of repairing stuff yourself, anyway—and he works fast.

—Peter Trice, Tester

Fire, Theft, and Accidents

You know the saying: "Crud happens." Life's not a bowl of cherries. And, darn it, we never promised you a rose garden, either. When you hit bumps in the road, both little and big, just remember: keep a stiff upper lip. And keep the following tips in mind.

Floods

No, the riverbanks won't overflow. But *The Sims'* manual labels "flood" any spills or leaks caused by sloppy Sims or accidents—broken appliances, bladder failure, and so forth. Naturally, Room score drops if a Sim must slog through puddles in, say, the kitchen.

When messy people get out of the tub or shower, or clean the aquarium, often they leave a puddle of water on one tile of the room. This puddle can grow, but only if there's further activity. For example, if a messy person steps out of a shower where a one-tile puddle already exists, it becomes a two-tile puddle. And so on. Bladder failure also leaves a one-tile flood. Any Sim denied access to bathroom facilities can suffer this monumental indignity.

> **NOTE**
> When directed to clean up one "flood tile" (one grid square of a spill), Sims continue to mop up all flooded tiles in the room unless interrupted by another command or if their Mood score drops below zero.

Floods created by appliance breakdowns are bigger, multi-tile spills. The puddle keeps growing as long as Sims keep using the source of the spill (say, a broken dishwasher) before it's repaired or removed. If you don't clean it up, a multi-tile spill evaporates only after two Sim days.

Fig. 7-12. Big floods mean appliance failure. Fix the broken item quickly, or risk more flooding and rock-bottom Room scores.

Fire

Only three types of objects can cause a fire in *The Sims*—fireplaces, stoves, and the Wild Bill THX-451 barbecue. Stoves and barbecues catch fire when unskilled cooks try to cook a meal. Fireplaces don't catch fire, but their sparks can set nearby objects ablaze. (Fire can't start on a floor tile.)

Fire spreads quickly to flammable objects (including people) on adjacent tiles, so get it under control fast. Fires also can spread to empty tiles, but the probability is less. While a fire burns, Buy and Build mode are disabled. Fires awaken any Sims sleeping in the same room.

Cooking Fires

Again, cooking fires can begin on a stovetop used by low-skilled cooks. Microwave ovens can't start fires, but chances are greatest that your Toaster oven will flame up. A Sim's chance of starting a cooking fire relates to skill value, thus:

Fig. 7-13. Poolside barbecues are fun, but that nearby plant and chair are poorly placed firetraps. Keep objects off tiles adjacent to barbecues and fireplaces.

COOKING SKILL POINTS	PERCENT CHANCE OF FIRE
0	15
1	5
2	1
3–10	0

Fireplace Fires

Be careful around fireplaces! If you build one, place no furniture or other objects on tiles adjacent to it. Fireplace fires break out only when objects are right next to a lit fireplace.

Panic and Extinguishing Fires

When a fire breaks out, the Panic interaction pushes to the front of everyone's queue. Unfortunately, Sims continue to panic as long as the fire burns; they won't pick any other interaction autonomously. Thus, Sims won't extinguish fires until you order the screaming fools to do so.

Fig. 7-14. Fire immediately sends Panic to the front of every nearby Sim's interaction queue. If you don't order someone to extinguish the flames, no one will.

In *The Sims*, each tile of a multi-tile blaze is considered an individual fire. Sims extinguish fires one tile at a time. When ordered to extinguish a fire, a Sim continues to extinguish individual outbreaks of the fire in adjacent tiles until no more fires remain. Careful! The Sim with the extinguisher can catch fire, too.

While extinguishing a fire, a Sim's Hygiene score drops precipitously to a limit of –50. If the Sim's Energy is less than zero, it will climb to a limit of 0. This prevents Sims from falling asleep right after the arduous task of putting out a fire . . . and really makes them want to bathe afterward.

Fire Damage

Flammable objects burn for approximately 75 seconds before turning into an ash pile. If a fire is extinguished before the object has turned to ash, the object is unharmed. As you might expect, Sims who catch fire go much quicker. If you don't extinguish a burning Sim within a few seconds, he or she becomes a lovely, well-crafted burial urn.

Tips from the Testers

Smoke alarms are cheap! Unless all your Sims have a Cooking skill of 4 or higher, you need a smoke alarm on the wall near your stove. If a fire starts in the kitchen, the Fire Department arrives automatically.

—Syruss Flyte, Tester

Calling the Fire Department

Your local Firefighter puts out fires faster than family members, and stays until the job's done. But don't make frivolous calls. If you call the Fire Department when no fire is burning, you get a lecture and a $100 fine.

Burglars

Burglars strike randomly when a house is empty or if everyone is asleep. They steal objects, starting with the most expensive, pilfering up to five objects in a session. Your best defense: buy a burglar alarm for each room of your house as soon as you can! Buy and Build modes are disabled during a burglary, so you can't just purchase a burglar alarm when the fiend appears, or quickly sell off objects to keep them safe.

Fig. 7-15. Smoke alarms in the kitchen bring Firefighters running at the first sign of a blaze.

When your alarm sounds, the Police arrive on the scene quickly. (You can try to call the Police if you don't have an alarm, but the cop rarely arrives in time.) If the Police Officer arrives while the burglar is still on the premises, the cop almost always catches his or her man. The cop also confiscates stolen items as evidence. But not only do you get simoleans from your insurance company to replace the stolen goods (based on their depreciated value when stolen), but you also get a §1,000 cash reward. Sweet!

Be aware that if you call the Police when no burglar is in house, the cop scolds you about false alarms. Unlike false fire alarms, however, this transgression carries no fine. Cops, apparently, are more forgiving.

Fig. 7-16. Cops catch crooks regularly only if you make burglar alarms priority purchases.

Tips from the Testers

The best place for a burglar alarm is next to the portals where Sims enter and exit the lots. Placing burglar alarms indoors can be iffy, because once the burglar starts running, the cop can't catch him. Placing alarms on a wall segment at lot corners will alert the Police the moment the burglar steps into the lot; cops will catch the burglar every time, and give you §1,000 for the catch.

And here's another tip. Two Sims can corral the burglar until the cops arrive. Have one Sim call the Police and direct the other to stand on the tile next to the front door. The burglar will route to the back door (if there is one). Now hustle and stand on the tile next to the back door. (Slow the burglar by keeping your cursor over him.) The burglar will route back to the front door. Repeat until the Police Officer shows up. If you have only one door, you can still slow the burglar by trying to get in the way, but the cad will get through eventually.

Fig. 7-17.Tips for the Truly Paranoid: Install burglar alarms on single wall panels at lot corners. Detect thieves before they even reach the house.

—Andrew Blomquist, Tester

8
Building

Building a dwelling can (and should) be a highly creative act of personal expression. This is particularly true when the builder has access to the kinds of tools you find in *The Sims*. So we hesitate to offer you "strategies" for constructing your own dreams (or nightmares). Who knows better how to do that than you?

Of course, we can offer some simple, common sense sort of guidelines. This section reiterates many of the Quick Tips embedded in *The Sims* in-game Help System. We also pass along a few fun tips from those twisted EA testers. But, in general, our advice is *go for it*. That's the real beauty of Will Wright's philosophy of game design. His goal: put the creative tools in your hands and let *you* be the game designer.

Fig. 8-1. Remodel existing homes or build from scratch on an empty lot. Either way, THE SIMS construction tools are easy to use.

> **NOTE**
> Visit *www.thesims.com* regularly to download more floor patterns and wall textures for your construction and remodeling projects, or get tools for creating your own.

Tips from the Testers

Resist the urge to build too big. In a huge home, your Sims waste far too much time just walking around. The best tactic for expanding your house is to increase the size of your rooms incrementally (adding better windows, wallpaper, floors, and furnishings) only until the Room score is maxed out. This way you have all of the benefits of a large house, but your Sims won't have to spend half an hour walking from the fridge to the table.

—Andrew Blomquist, Tester

A Special Note on Remodeling

Before we discuss building options, let's reiterate an important point we made in the previous section about *un*building options. One of the great joys of *The Sims* is the ease with which you can remodel existing homes. Tear out a wall here, add floor space there, scrape off that ugly Hollywood Hills mauve stucco and replace it with something elegant, rip up old, cheap carpeting and lay down some gorgeous hardwood or gray shale flooring. What a blast!

Fig. 8-2. If you decide to remodel, be sure to strip off old wall and floor coverings (interior and exterior) for the depreciated cash refund before putting on the new stuff.

TIP

Always remove old paint or wallpaper before repainting a room to get some of your original investment back. Do the same with floor tiles —delete old tiles before placing new ones.

In the rush to remodel, however, players sometimes forget that their old walls and floors are worth simoleans. Yes, materials depreciate over time, but their value never drops below 80 percent of their initial cost. (See "Build Depreciation" in chapter 7, "Sim Economics 101".) However, if you just cover over existing tiles, the old stuff just disappears, *poof*, no cash back.

The point: *always delete used floor and wall coverings as the first step in remodeling!* This sells the old stuff back and adds funds to your remodeling budget.

Architecture Items

What follows is a quick review of some Build mode basics.

Undo/Redo Items

Fig. 8-3. Oops. That diagonal balustrade looks pretty stupid. Just hit the Undo button to wipe it from your design slate.

Mistakes happen. Hey, even Frank Lloyd Wright had regrets. Too bad he didn't have an Undo button. During any building session you can click the Undo icon to reverse the last change you made (and get *all* your money back). Keep clicking it to undo previous changes. Once you leave Build mode, however, your changes become permanent. After that, you can delete them, but you'll lose some money to depreciation.

Selling Items

If it's too late for Undo, you can get money back for most architectural items by deleting or selling them. Things you can pick up you can delete using the Hand tool. Other architectural tools have more specific instructions. Click a selection's thumbnail under each tool to learn how to delete it.

Fig. 8-4. When in doubt about how to place or delete any architectural item, just click on its thumbnail to get directions (and a full description of the item).

Rotating/Moving Items

You can use the Hand tool to delete, move, or rotate many architectural items, free of charge.

Terrain Tools

Hills are interesting. Dales aren't bad, either. Or maybe you want a boggy, mosquito-breeding trench ringing your property. *The Sims* terrain tools let you raise and lower earth with abandon. And the way-cool "water_tool" cheat gives you additional landscaping options.

Here's a look at the basics of terrain adjustment.

Level

You need level ground for most objects and all Sim-to-Sim interactions. To create flat ground, click on the Level Terrain tool, and then click-and-drag out a rectangle. The land in the rectangle becomes the same height as the spot where you first clicked the mouse. Grass will grow back by itself over time.

Fig. 8-5. The Level Terrain tool

Hilly

As you probably deduced, the Raise Terrain tool raises terrain. Just click or click-and-drag to raise terrain level. But here's a little tip. If you hold down [Control] as you raise terrain, the tool goes nuts and you can make some nice curvy hills.

Fig. 8-6. The Raise Terrain tool

The Water Tool Cheat

We told you about this cheat earlier in chapter 1, "Cheats and Quick Start Tips," but we mention it again here because it's just so darn neat. Press [Control][Shift][C] to bring up the Cheat window, then type in water_tool. Now you can add dramatic ponds, quiet creeks, sibilant streams, or wet, festering peat bogs to your property. Just remember, your Sims can't route through water.

Fig. 8-7. We routed this lovely meandering stream past our brownstone cottage, adding some indigenous greenery to create a peaceful garden setting.

Plant Tool

Landscaping the grounds is so easy, we have little to say about the tool itself. Just click to place plants, flowers, and trees where you want them. Move or delete them with the Hand tool. That's it. But keep the following, very helpful tips in mind.

Effect of Outdoor Plants on Room Score

Outdoor plants raise your Sims' appreciation of an area and thus improve their Room scores. Remember, everything outdoors on the lot is considered one big room. EA tester Andrew Blomquist says, "The outside Room score is very important, because Sims are always outside before they go to work. Make sure you build a lot of room for your Sims and plant lots of trees."

Fellow tester Syruss Flyte agrees, adding, "Put plenty of flowers, shrubs, a fountain, and so forth in the yard. As Sims walk to the car pool, they'll get a big Room score boost. This helps raise their mood and, hence, their job performance rating."

But, of course, if flowers or flowering bushes aren't cared for, they'll die. If your Sims don't have time to look after flowering plants, prepare to spend money on a Gardener.

Flower Care

Flowers start as buds. They follow a six-day cycle: if you don't water them, they wilt in three days, and die in three more. Dead flowers, of course, will push your Sims' Room scores in the negative direction. Note that you can water wilted flowers before they die. Watering wilted flowers is free and thus much less expensive than replacing a patch of dead flowers with a new purchase.

When you direct a Sim to water a patch of outdoor flowers, he or she will continue watering *all* outdoor flowers unless you insert another command in the queue, or until the Sim's mood falls below –50.

By the way, stomping on blooming flowers makes them wilt; if they've wilted already, or haven't yet bloomed, a good stomping kills them dead. Note that Sims stomp autonomously only if their mood is low. You cannot direct them to do it.

Plant Trees for Ease

Yes, you must water flowers regularly. Trees and shrubs, however, require no maintenance: they never wilt or die, yet they add roughly the same to your Room score as flowers do. So tree-planting is a good way to boost outside Room score without the expense of hiring a Gardener or spending precious time watering plants yourself. Of course, trees are more expensive than flowers.

Wall Tool

Walls are kind of important to a house. They hold up the roof, among other things. In *The Sims*, they also become the crux of the privacy issue.

The Privacy Issue

Consider two things when you design your room layout. First, Sims need privacy to perform bathroom functions. A Sim won't bathe or use the toilet, regardless of Bladder or Hygiene scores, if another Sim is in the bathroom, unless the two Sims have a "love" relationship. (To Sims, bladder accidents are preferable to being seen using a toilet. Go figure.) Second, Sims can't sleep if noisy objects such as TVs, stereos, pinball machines, computers, or exercise machines are being used in the same room. So your bedroom best be enclosed.

Fig. 8-8. Bathroom privacy is a design issue you can't escape, no matter how modern you feel. Bedrooms should be enclosed as well, to avoid unwanted wake-ups.

Drag Out Rooms

Here's just a little reminder. You can build a complete room in one fell swoop by holding down [Shift] as you drag out a wall. Keep [Shift] pressed until you release the mouse button.

Removing Walls

To delete a wall, hold down [Ctrl]. The wall cursor changes to a wrecking ball. Then draw over the existing wall to remove it. Be sure to hold [Ctrl] down until you've released the mouse button.

Fig. 8-9. Shift-click and drag out walls to create entire rooms in one smooth motion.

TIP

Make it easier for your Sims to navigate through the house by leaving at least two grid squares between walls.

Diagonal Walls

Sims like *roomy* rooms with lots of corners. The more corners, the better. So slice the corners off rectangular spaces with diagonal wall sections. (See Figure 8-10.) Diagonal walls can make the house look a little nicer, too. Don't overdo it, though. You can't place doors, windows, or objects on or against diagonal walls.

Fig. 8-10. The bay window nook in this house-in-progress not only looks nice, but its diagonal walls add more corners to the room, boosting your Sim's Room score.

TIP

Sims like big rooms. And the more corners the better.

Columns

You can place columns with the Wall tool, as well. Using columns as support, you can build a second-story deck or, our favorite, a catwalk connecting stone turrets ringing the perimeter of our "compound." (We've always wanted a compound.) Each column supports a 3-by-3-tile floor area, so a second-floor deck can extend five tiles out.

Floor Tool

You don't have to waste time placing one floor tile at a time. Click-and-drag to place a rectangle of tiles, or hold down (Shift) and click to cover the whole room at once. The reverse is true, too. To remove a rectangle of tiles, hold down (Ctrl) and then click-and-drag. To remove an entire room's flooring, hold down (Ctrl)(Shift), and then click on any tile in the room.

CAUTION

Sims become quite displeased with unfinished rooms, as you might expect. If you overspend on wall space and don't leave enough funds for wall or floor coverings, watch that Room score plummet! Of course, it's also good to note that Sims have no preference for wall or floor coverings—they just care that they are covered.

When removing a rectangle of tiles, be sure to release the mouse button *before* you release [Ctrl]. If you reverse that order (releasing [Ctrl] first, mouse button second), the floor tool will place the selected tile pattern on the rectangle you've dragged out instead of removing the existing floor tiles.

Wallpaper Tool

You don't have to place wall covering one strip at a time. You can paint or wallpaper a whole room by holding down [Shift] and clicking the left mouse button. Holding down [Shift] is also a nice way to preview how the room's walls will look with the selected covering.

To remove a wall's paint or wallpaper, hold down [Ctrl] while using the Wallpaper tool. To clear a whole room, hold down [Ctrl] [Shift], and then click the Wallpaper tool on the wall.

Doors and Windows

Door Tool

Doors are one of life's unsung essentials. They let you come and go, of course. But in *The Sims*, most doors can provide light, too. Along with increasing a room's size, light is one of the best ways to improve a Sims' feeling about a room—that is, raise their Room motive scores.

TIP

Doors are a single tile wide. To create lovely double doors, place them side by side and rotate them using the < > keys.

Don't waste money on installing doors unless the room is totally enclosed. Sims won't use a door if there's any other access to a room. If a room isn't enclosed, don't enclose it with objects. Even if there is a door, your Sims will not enter the room.

How to Delete Doors

To delete doors, select the Door tool and hold down [Ctrl]. The cursor becomes the Delete icon (a circle with slash through it). Move the Delete icon over the door you want to remove. When that door is highlighted, click to remove it.

A deleted door is replaced by a section of wall covered by the paint or wallpaper on the surrounding wall. Note that you also can remove a door by using the Wall tool to draw a wall over it. The result is the same as if you removed it using the Delete icon.

Fig. 8-11. Doors are more than just access portals in The Sims. Paned models like the Monticello add necessary light to a room, too.

Window Tool

Sims like rooms with lots of light. The bigger the room, the more windows it takes to brighten it during the day. Note that all windows give the same amount of light whether large or small.

How to Delete Windows

To delete windows, select the Window tool and hold down Ctrl. The cursor becomes the Delete icon. Move the Delete icon over the window you want to remove. When that window is highlighted, click to remove it.

Tips from the Testers

If you're feeling sadistic, or just want to get rid of those annoying visiting Sims, build a swimming pool moat all the way around your house. On the resulting "island," put ladders into the pool, and on the outside edge of the pool put only a diving board.

When unsuspecting neighbors come over to visit, they dive into the pool and climb out onto the island. When these visitors leave, they climb back into the pool, but have no way to get back out—except to return to Death Island. Eventually, trapped neighbors die of starvation. You can acquire an impressive cemetery on your lawn this way.

—Syruss Flyte, Tester

Fig. 8-12. We tried Syruss Flyte's perverse "human trap" moat. It worked beautifully, man. Here we see four neighbors starving in the pool/moat.

Fig. 8-13. And here we see the final results—six gravestones on Death Island, and no more solicitors.

A deleted window is replaced by a section of wall covered by the paint or wallpaper decorating the surrounding wall tile. You also can remove a window by using the Wall tool to draw a wall over it. The result is the same as if you removed it using the Delete icon.

Water Tool (Swimming Pool)

Swimming in a pool improves your Sim's Fun score, and it has the side benefit of improving Body skill. Sims can use the pool ladder to Get In or the diving board to Dive In. Exit is impossible without a ladder, however. As mentioned, swimming builds Body skill points, but not as quickly as working out on the Exerto exercise machine. Also, swimming doesn't follow the usual skill development rules; for example, a Sim needn't be in a good mood to swim.

TIP

Swimming is *not* a group activity. Multiple Sims in a pool have fun, but earn no Social or Relationship points.

Stairs

Stairs connect the first story to the second. When placing stairs, they automatically cut a hole in the second floor. You can place stairs outside, as well, to connect to balconies; just make sure they connect to a floor tile on the second story.

Second Story

The transparent grid on the second story represents tiles the first-story construction supports. These are the only areas on the second story where you can place floor tiles and walls. Use columns to extend this area, if you like.

9
Sim
Objects

H ere it is—the big honkin' section you've been waiting for. Objects! Dozens of them! Lined up in neat catalog rows, all there for the taking—if you have the simoleans, that is. Plus, we've included detailed descriptions of all the new objects added to the game in the *Livin' Large* expansion pack.

We open with some notes about how Sim objects are appraised, repaired, sold, moved, and so on. Then we review all the new *Livin' Large* objects. Finally, we provide an exhaustive rundown of the game's other catalog items and objects, in alphabetical order. Use it as a handy A-to-Z Sims shopping guide.

NOTE

Visit *www.thesims.com* regularly to download more new catalog items.

How Sims Appraise New Purchases

Sims can be snobs. Each new item bought and placed in a Sim household broadcasts a "Come and See Me" message. Sim residents respond by examining the object and expressing a response—positive (clap), negative ("uh-uh" and a red X through the object), or indifferent (shrug). The quality of the stuff they already own modifies this response. The more expensive their current stuff, the less likely they are to find new stuff very exciting.

See? Snobbery.

Here's how it works. a Sims response to new objects relates to the average value of all objects in the household. The game takes the following steps:

Fig. 9-1. This fellow likes his new computer desk. Reaction to a new object is based on a formula that compares its value to the average value of a Sim's other stuff. The more expensive the new item, the more likely the Sim is to approve of the purchase.

- Calculates the average value for all objects in the household.
- Subtracts 10 percent of the new object's value for each copy of the same object that exists. (Sims don't get as excited about the third large-screen TV as they did for the first.)
- Compares values.
- If the new object's value is more than 20 percent above the average value for all objects, your Sim claps a positive response.
- If the new object is less than 20 percent below the average value for all objects, your Sim waves a negative response.
- If the new object is between 20 percent above or below the average value for all objects, your Sim shrugs an indifferent response.

Repairing Broken Objects

When something breaks, a Sim can either fix the item or call the neighborhood Repair service. Even Sims with zero Mechanical points can repair a broken object; low and high skill levels are equally effective at repair. But repairs by low-skill Sims take much, much longer. If you have the cash, call a Repairman. Spend the time you save doing something more productive. Napping, for instance.

TIP

The game "remembers" the amount of repair work done on a broken item. If a Sim spends time repairing an object and gets interrupted, the object will need less repair time when any Sim returns to finish the job.

Buy Mode

Ah, Buy mode. It sounds so American, doesn't it? Here's where you indulge your acquisitive nature, loading up on consumer goods without leaving the comfort of your computer nook.

The Object Catalog

Online catalogs are fun, aren't they? Easy to use, easy to go broke. The one in *The Sims* is no different. To see a larger version of each catalog item, click its thumbnail. You'll also get a description and a rating of the object's usefulness.

Objects may be grouped for viewing by function or by room. Click the Buy Mode button or press F2 to toggle between them.

Function is the default grouping. This is probably the easiest way to find objects after you've furnished a home. But when you move into a new place, it's probably easier to group objects by room. As you fill each empty room, it's convenient to view the catalog items for that room only.

Fig. 9-2. You may group catalog items by function or by room.

Rotating/Moving Objects

After your catalog buying spree, it's easy to rearrange household objects. To move an object, click on it once (the tiles beneath it highlight yellow), drag it to a new location, and click again to put it down. To rotate an object, click and hold down the mouse button as you drag it where you want.

Selling Objects

To sell an object, click on it once, and then either drag it back to the Control Panel or press ⌊Delete⌋. If you sell the object back before midnight on the day it is bought, you'll get all your money back. After you've had an object for a while, its value goes down. Certain objects may increase in value over time. (For more on object depreciation and appreciation, see "Object Depreciation" in chapter 7, "Sim Economics 101.")

New Interactive Objects in LIVIN' LARGE

The *Livin' Large* expansion pack adds dozens of new decorative and functional objects to your Sim catalog—chairs, tables, sofas, beds, lamps, appliances, paintings, and sculptures, plus a whole lot of other stuff. Most of these are "mimic" objects—that is, they function the same way as similar objects already in the game. You sit in chairs, sleep in beds, and view art objects. *All* chairs boost Comfort, *all* beds raise Energy, *all* art objects add Room points, and so forth.

But *Livin' Large* also adds whimsical new items that feature new interactions—some with really wild and unpredictable consequences. In this section we give you a complete description of what each new object does.

Fig. 9-3. The LIVIN' LARGE expansion pack adds a number of new interactive objects to THE SIMS.

> **NOTE**
> Livin' Large also adds the Grim Reaper and Tragic Clown as new interactive gameplay characters. To learn how the Reaper functions, see "Death" in chapter 3, "Moods and Motives." We discuss the Clown later in this section.

Roaches (Free)

Spawned from dirty objects such as trash, dishes, ashes, tubs, and unmade beds, roaches really put a damper on your Room score. Sim autonomously stomp on roach swarms or, if they're particularly Neat Sims, just freak out. (The Neater the Sim, the longer they freak out.) None of this stomping or panicking does much good, however. The only way to eliminate roaches is to click on the swarm and select "Spray." Note that this is not so easy; roach swarms move from tile to tile quickly. In fact, it is almost impossible to click on roaches in any but the slowest time setting.

Fig. 9-4. Go ahead, stomp all you want. But you can't kill roach swarms unless you "Spray" them.

Viva PGT Home Casino (§1,750)

Yes, the Viva PGT Home Casino brings the wholesome sport of gambling right into your living room. Just pop your money into the slot—you can gamble either §10 or §100 (unless, of course, you don't have enough simoleans in your account)—pull the handle, and watch destiny take a whirl.

Interestingly enough, Sims' chances of winning are directly affected by their current Fun level. The lower the Fun motive, the greater the odds of winning. When Fun is bottomed out at –100, you have a 1 in 3 chance of

Fig. 9-5. The lower your Fun motive, the better your chance of winning the Home Casino jackpot.

winning. When Fun is at a robust 100, the odds drop to a long shot 1 in 30. Between these two extremes, the odds increase in a linear fashion.

When you hit the jackpot, the payout is 10 to 1. So a low bet earns you §100, and a high bet earns §1,000. Winning also gives your Fun motive a healthy boost, which makes perfect sense. Losing, on the other hand, doesn't affect your Fun motive.

Fig. 9-6. Sure, he's cute. But he's also a germ-bag. If you don't keep your guinea pig cage clean, the beast can bite and spread a deadly disease.

Guinea Pig (§120)

Guinea pigs can be cute, furry little bundles of joy—fun to watch, hold, and play with. It's even fun to watch other Sims play with a guinea pig, which leads to Group Talk interactions. (See "Group Talk" in chapter 5, "Social Interactions.")

Unfortunately, guinea pigs can also be diseased little vermin, spreading sickness throughout your Sim household. It's up to you. Clean the cage regularly or risk suffering an infectious bite from an unclean rodent.

Once Sims catch the guinea pig disease, they get progressively sicker, proceeding from mild illness (a few coughs and an occasional sneeze) to severe illness (more fits of sneezing and coughing) to a visit from your friendly neighborhood Grim Reaper.

> **NOTE**
> Don't overfeed your guinea pig. The creature needs only one meal per day. If you feed it too much, you accelerate the rate the pig soils its cage.

How to Cure the Guinea Pig Disease

Fortunately, there are three ways to completely heal a stricken Sim.

1. Purchase "The Forgotten Guinea Pig" painting, hang it on a wall, and let it magically cure the disease within 16 hours.

2. Direct the diseased Sim (must be an adult) to make potions with the "Concatenation Station" Home Chemistry Lab (see next section) until achieving a white potion. Drink the white potion to cure the disease.

3. Then there's the old-fashioned way—*get lots of bed rest*. Keep your Energy score up, and after a while that cold and cough will disappear.

Fig. 9-7. When guinea pig disease strikes, one recourse is to buy "The Forgotten Guinea Pig" painting. It's incredibly ugly, but it cures the illness.

 TIP

If you don't have a lot of time to sleep off the guinea pig disease, purchase an espresso machine or coffeemaker to boost that Energy. Again, high Energy scores heal sick Sims.

"The Concatenation Station" Home Chemistry Lab (§980)

Adults only. Builds Logic skill. The first use offers the interaction "Make Potion"— the Sim using the chemistry set brews one of eight random potions. The next use offers the interaction "Drink Potion"—that is, you cannot make another potion until an adult Sim drinks the potion last made.

Fig. 9-8. Make wild potions with this chemistry set.

All potions have an equal chance of being made except for the blue potion, which always has a four times greater chance of being made, and the white potion, a cure for the Guinea Pig Disease, is available only if the Sim who makes the potion is sick. Each potion, when drunk, spawns a different reaction. The eight potions and their reactions are:

Blue: Motive Enhancer

This potion maxes out all motives—Hunger, Energy, Comfort, Hygiene, Fun, Bladder, Social, and Room. As mentioned earlier, Sims are four times more likely to make this blue potion. However, there is a 1 in 3 chance that a Sim drinking this potion during the day (before 6 p.m.) will get busted by police and fined §500 for "creating mysterious substances." (Motives stay maxed, however—not even *cops* can take motives away from you.)

Chartreuse: Motive Subtractor

This potion produces the opposite effect of the blue potion. When imbibed, chartreuse potions make the Sim feel absolutely terrible, dropping all motive scores to extremely low levels. (Hunger doesn't drop *all* the way to the bottom, of course, because that would be a mortal blow.) Nonetheless, this is a very unpleasant drink.

Brown: Invisibility

Any adult Sim who drinks this potion turns invisible for one glorious hour. Of course, you see the Sim as semitransparent vapor, and you can still direct their actions. Invisible Sims can perform all interactions, including social interactions with other Sims. One crucial benefit—you can spy on other Sims taking baths, showers, and so forth. However, other Sims can't initiate social interactions with invisible Sims because they can't see them.

Red: Love

This potion causes the Sim drinker and his or her worst enemy (lowest Relationship score) of the opposite gender to fall in love with each other. In fact, *The Sims* teleports the new lover directly to the Sim drinker's side for a quick romantic interlude. That's just one more reason why this game is a classic.

Green: Evil Clone

Any Sim who drinks this potion gets the message: "It's a parthenogenesis party! [Your Sim's Name] has created an evil clone!" Sim and clone have opposite personality traits. (Skills remain the same, however.) Clones hang out and slap, insult, and annoy you and other Sims for six Sim hours, which in turn lowers your relationships with your established friends.

Every half hour, a social interaction is "pushed" on the clone, directed either toward the original Sim (from whom the clone is spawned) or toward someone else on the lot. The clone insults, slaps, or even attacks its progenitor.

Yellow: Personality Inversion

When your Sim drinks a yellow potion, you get the message: "Holy inverse proportionality! Your personality has been permanently reversed!" Yes, all six personality traits get flipped to their opposite value—for example, a Neat rating of 10 becomes 0, 9 becomes 1, 8 becomes 2, 7 becomes 3, and so on.

Pink: Monster

Yes, drinking the pink potion turns a Sim into a clumsy sort of Frankenstein's monster for two Sim hours. During this time, the monster ignores your commands and lumbers about the house, breaking everything that's breakable—appliances, plumbing, electronics, whatever it can get its grubby green hands on.

Fig. 9-9. The pink potion really brings out the monster in a gal. Here, Miss FrankenSim breaks the dishwasher, then clogs up the bathroom shower and sink.

White: Cure (Diseased Sims Only)

If a Sim who has contracted the dreaded guinea pig disease uses the chemistry lab, *The Sims* adds the white potion as an optional brew. Drinking this concoction immediately wipes out the disease. It's a 1 in 11 long shot to produce, though, so your best bet is to buy "The Forgotten Guinea Pig" painting. This cures your Sims within 16 Sim hours.

The Vibromatic Heart Bed (§4,500)

This new bed not only boosts Comfort with its sensuous "Relax" and "Vibrate" interactions; it also lets a consenting pair of lovers "Play in Bed." To engage in play, one Sim must get the bed vibrating first. Then that Sim crawls in and can invite a lover to "Play in Bed." Or you can select the lover and choose "Play in Bed," but only while the bed is still occupied and vibrating.

Note also that the occupied, vibrating bed advertises *very* highly to anyone in love with the occupant, including visitors. Therefore, an invitation or command isn't always necessary; the lover just hops right in.

> **NOTE**
>
> No more than two Sims can play in bed at a time, and the pair must be in love. Isn't that quaint?

Fig. 9-10. Care to play? LIVIN' LARGE has just the bed for you.

In any case, this bed play has several consequences. It gives a considerable boost to the participants' Fun and Social motives, as well as their mutual Relationship scores. The activity also carries a 1 in 8 chance of producing a baby. As you might expect, this sort of exuberant play also makes Energy, Hunger, and Hygiene drop like rocks.

Antique Lamp (With Genie) (§375)

Adults only. Can be used only once per day. Two interactions: "View" and "Clean." The first adult Sim who cleans the lamp each day summons a genie. Unfortunately, he's not a very good genie. Although he has the power to cast spells, they go horribly wrong about 60 percent of the time.

Fig. 9-11. Meet the genie. He has some good spells in his repertoire—but he's awfully rusty. In fact, about 60 percent of the spells go bad.

When he appears, the genie asks you to choose between two types of spells. Each spell has a success outcome and a failure outcome. The spell pairings are:

> **TIP**
>
> Save your game before you summon the genie each time. His spells gone bad can be a real downward drag on your upward mobility.

- Friends/Family
- Fire/Water
- Money/Love
- Work/Leisure
- Earth/Air

Friends Spell

The genie picks a random acquaintance (not a friend), or, if your Sim has no acquaintances, he finds a neighbor you haven't met. (If your Sim is alone in the neighborhood, the genie says, "Nice try, sneaky Sim! You don't have any friends or neighbors.") The game auto-centers on the chosen Sim if he or she is visiting the household; otherwise, the genie teleports the Sim nearby.

Good Outcome: The genie sets the Relationship score to 60 between your Sim and the chosen acquaintance, pushing it above the 50-point friendship threshold. The genie also raises all of your new friend's motives to 70 except Social, which is dropped to –50. This guarantees a good mood but makes the new friend hungry for social interactions, most likely with positive results.

Bad Outcome: The genie accidentally finds your Sim's best friend (based on highest Relationship score) and lowers the Relationship score to –55. If the Sim has no friends, the genie picks a random Sim in the neighborhood and lowers that Sim's Relationship score by 20 points. Bladder, Fun, Hygiene, Energy, and Comfort motives are set to –15; Hunger is set to –40; and Social drops clear to the bottom at –100. This volatile combination usually leads to emotional fireworks, as you can imagine.

Family Spell

If your Sim has no family members—that is, no housemates in the current household—then the genie says, "If you *had* a family I might be able to help you out, foolish one!"

Good outcome: The genie adds 20 Relationship points to all family members and cycles through them, pushing a "Compliment" toward your Sim to the front of their queue.

Bad outcome: The genie accidentally *subtracts* 20 Relationship points to all family members and cycles through them, pushing an "Insult" toward your Sim to the front of their queue.

Work Spell

Good outcome: The genie adds one point apiece to three different skills chosen randomly.

Bad outcome: The genie accidentally subtracts one point from every skill in which the Sim has earned at least one point.

Leisure Spell

Good outcome: The genie makes a Fun object suddenly appear, choosing randomly from among the pinball machine, pool table, train set, and the Soma large-screen TV.

Bad outcome: The genie accidentally sets fire to the household object with the highest value.

Money Spell

Good outcome: The genie zaps you a pile of gold worth anywhere between §350 and §3,500.

Bad outcome: The genie accidentally conjures up several piles of unpaid bills. You must pay all of them.

Love Spell

First, the genie asks which gender you prefer, then he finds all Sims in the neighborhood who are of the chosen gender *and* not in love with the Sim summoner. From that subset, the genie selects the one with the highest Relationship score with his Sim summoner and teleports that Sim to your side.

Good outcome: The genie boosts the Relationship score between the two Sims to a full 100 points, raises all motives for both Sims to 80, and makes the teleported Sim fall in love with your active character. A passionate "Kiss" is pushed to the front of the interaction queue.

Bad outcome: The genie accidentally decreases the Relationship between the Sims by 50 points and knocks all motive scores down to –15, creating some bad feelings. A crisp "Slap" gets pushed to the front of the interaction queue.

Earth Spell

Good outcome: The genie bestows full health and watering on all plants, indoor and outdoor. If the Sim has no plants, the genie conjures up three healthy indoor plants.

Bad outcome: The genie accidentally kills all indoor and outdoor plants. If the Sim has no plants, the genie conjures up five dead indoor plants.

Air Spell

Good outcome: The genie bestows 10 pink lawn flamingoes on the lucky Sim. What a fabulous bonus.

Bad outcome: The genie accidentally bestows nine swarms of roaches on the not-so-lucky Sim. Fortunately, they usually appear in the same room, making it easier to spray and kill them off.

Fire Spell

Good outcome: The genie sets the Comfort and Social motives of all Sims in the household to a glowing green 100 percent.

Bad outcome: The genie accidentally sets a flammable object on fire.

Horrorwitz "Star-Track" Backyard Telescope (§2,100)

Motive: Fun. Also increases Logic skill and, for Sim kids, school grades. Must be placed outside. But the real fun is the random chance that, while stargazing, a Horrorwitz user will get abducted by aliens. Sim abductees disappear for six to twelve hours, then suddenly reappear, collapsed on the ground. They return with a randomly scrambled personality—the result, of course, of insidious alien probing and fiendish experimentation. Worse, an abducted Sim's conversation interests are completely reset to a single topic: *aliens.*

Fig. 9-12. Gaze at the stars, build Logic skill, raise your grades (if a kid)—but watch out for those darned "close encounters."

KraftKing Woodworking Table (§720)

Increases Mechanical skill. Makes garden gnomes only. The higher a Sim's Mechanical skill, the faster and better that Sim can crank out gnomes. By "better" we mean "worth more simoleans." Because once your Sim whittles a gnome out of a block of wood, it can be "sold" back to the game for cash. For more details on this, see the next section, "Garden Gnome."

Garden Gnome

Made with the KraftKing Woodworking Table (see previous section). Visitors in a bad mood may autonomously kick a gnome. But they'll get a surprise; the gnome explodes, knocking the visitors down. The explosion lowers the kicker's Hygiene, Comfort, and Fun motives. It also triggers the delayed explosion of any other gnome within a two-tile radius. Fortunately, gnome explosions don't start fires or leave any ash residue.

Fig. 9-13. The KraftKing Woodworking Table builds your Mechanical skill as you build enough gnomes to populate Rhode Island.

> **NOTE**
> The "Kick Gnome" interaction advertises only to neighbors who visit. Household Sims, no matter how grumpy, don't get the opportunity to kick a gnome autonomously.

As mentioned in the previous section, you can sell garden gnomes for extra simoleans. The formula for gnome worth is as follows. Note that when the number is 0, round up to 1.

Mechanical skill when starting work on gnome

×

Mechanical skill when finished making gnome

=

Number of simoleans gnome is worth

For example, if a Sim with a Mechanical skill of 3 starts making a gnome and finishes with a Mechanical Skill of 4, the gnome would be worth 12 simoleans.

Madame Blahbatfry Crystal Ball (§760)

Adult use only. The crystal ball can't be used until you place a chair next to it, facing the ball. Then each household Sim can use it only once per day. When adult Sims choose to "Gaze" into the crystal ball, they receive a cryptic riddle. This riddle refers to a particular personality trait and must be "solved" in the next 24 Sim hours. If you succeed, your Sim gains a point of that personality trait. If you fail, your Sim loses a point of that trait.

Fig. 9-14. The crystal ball is one of the only personality "cheats" in the game. By solving its riddles you add points to various traits.

Here are all riddles and solutions, listed by personality trait.

Playful Riddles

Playful riddles trigger the game to calculate the average hourly change in fun over a 24-hour period. Sims who have boosted their Fun score by an average of 13 points per hour during that day gain a point of the Playful trait. If the average Fun score doesn't raise at all, they lose a point of the trait. Sims who manage to raise their Fun score just a little neither gain nor lose a Playful point.

All of the Playful riddles are listed below.

Some spirits are down
Distraction is the attraction
Vision fun not frowns.

The child plays to smile
The adult plays for style
The wise play for themselves.

Sometimes just enjoying yourself is the greatest hurdle to jump. You can't grow as a person unless you let go once in a while.

Nice Riddles

Nice riddles trigger the game to compare the sum of all of the Sim's relationship values at the beginning and the end of the 24-hour period. If the sum increases by 10 points from beginning to end, you succeed and your Sim gains one point of the Nice trait. If the sum stays the same or decreases, you fail and your Sim loses one point of the trait. If the sum increases but by less than 10 points, the Sim's Nice trait stays the same.

All of the Nice riddles are listed below.

There was a young Sim without friend
Who's loneliness was without end
On the phone she did get
Many friends were then met
You should make yourself part of this trend.

Some Sims act mean every day
Being cruel is their form of play
They can't stand to act nice
Being mean it's a vice
Act kind to your friends or you'll pay.

Some manners can only be taught
Some think these can be bought
If you are uncouth and unkind
You may soon come to find
Your niceness has come to naught.

Active Riddles

Active riddles trigger the game to calculate the average change in Comfort scores over the 24-hour period. If your Comfort stays the same or decreases only slightly, you neither gain nor lose an Active point. If overall Comfort decreased significantly during the day (indicating that the Sim hasn't spent much time sitting or sleeping), you succeed and your Sim gains a point of the Active personality trait. If your overall Comfort increased, you fail and your Sim loses a point of the trait.

All of the Active riddles are listed below.

Those who lack will soon become still. Those who are
moving find things improving.

Two Sims were arguing about action. One said, "Action is
moving." The other said, "Moving is action." Get moving
or your own action may be moving.

Man who does nothing will become nothing. Man who
does everything will become everything.

Outgoing Riddles

Outgoing riddles trigger the game to count the number of greeted visitors on the lot each hour during the 24-hour period. If the total number of "visitor hours" is 15 or more,

Fig. 9-15. To "solve" the Outgoing riddles you must greet neighbors and keep them around for a cumulative total (all visitors combined) of 15 hours.

you win. This can be any combination of numbers of visitors and hours—that is, it can be 15 visitors for one hour apiece, or one visitor for 15 hours.

It is said that when the going gets friendly, the outgoing get friends! Get enough friends over and you will be more outgoing!

The caterpillar asked the butterfly, "What is the outgoing way?" The butterfly said, "Many visitors turn the caterpillar into a butterfly on the inside."

A witch once said, "A neighborhood is small and narrow. They that befriend the neighborhood grow wide inside." Prove this quickly.

Neat Riddles

Neat riddles trigger the game to count the number of "dirty objects" at the end of the 24-hour period. Dirty objects include roaches, trash, and ash piles; dirty dishes, sinks, tubs, showers, toilets, or aquariums; broken appliances, spills, and unmade beds; dead flowers or houseplants (including gift flowers from visitors); old food; and full trash cans or trash compactors.

If the final number of dirty objects is zero, you succeed and your Sim gains one Neat trait point. If the number of dirty objects is 1, the game makes no change in the Sim's Neat trait. If the number of dirty objects is more than 1, you fail and your Sim loses a Neat trait point.

What is the color of clean? Show these true colors and you will be made clean.

One day, a house cried out, "Clean me! Clean me!" A Sim cleaned this house only to find himself the cleaned one.

When the dirty things are changed to clean, what does this mean for the cleaner? Can the clean become cleaner once cleaned?

Tragic Clown (via the "Tragic Clown" Painting)

Sims who buy the Tragic Clown painting run the risk of letting the actual Tragic Clown himself into their lives. This annoying fellow can destroy any sense of well-being your Sims have earned. This is Will Wright's personal contribution to the *Livin' Large* expansion pack. In the words of the Maxis design document, the Tragic Clown "is depressed and downtrodden, the personification of a rain cloud."

Fig. 9-16. This painting combined with a low overall household mood triggers the appearance of the Tragic Clown—one of the most annoying household "guests" ever.

The clown appears in any home that has the Tragic Clown painting and whose family has an average Mood score of –20 or less. But unlike other guests, the clown won't leave. In fact, once he shows up, it's very difficult to get him out of the house. He mopes around, gets in the way, wails at his portrait, complains, and—worst of all—wakes your Sims whenever they try to sleep. The clown uses no household objects, suffers no motive decay, needs no sleep himself, and his reaction to every interaction is always the same— uncontrollable sobbing.

Clown Tricks

The clown occasionally tries to perform one of three pathetic tricks.

1. Balloon animals: Stretches a balloon, blows it up, starts to fold it. The balloon breaks or pops at one of these three points in the trick.

2. Juggling pins: Inevitably, one of the pins hits him on the head. *Owwww!*

3. Dove in handkerchief: Clown pulls the handkerchief away, the bird starts to flap away—then drops like a rock.

Fig. 9-17. The clown's aggressively tragic demeanor can slowly erode your family's motives.

But if you think you can outsmart the clown by sealing him in a room with no portals—well, forget it. He has one other trick, and this one actually works. Whenever the clown faces a "routing failure"—that is, he can't get where he wants to go—he simply plops a hole onto the tile where he stands, hops in, then emerges elsewhere on the lot. So you can't trap the fool either.

How to Get Rid of the Clown

Once the Tragic Clown appears, selling or deleting the Tragic Clown painting will not eliminate his presence. Fortunately, there are two ways to rid yourself of the pest.

1. Hang the Tragic Clown painting over a fireplace and remove any smoke alarms from the room. (You don't want the Fire Department to come right away.) Keep lighting the fireplace until it goes out of control and starts a house fire. Let the fire burn (constantly directing your panicking Sims away from the flames) until the painting catches on fire. As the Tragic Clown painting burns, the Tragic Clown burns, too. Once he disappears, extinguish the flames or call the Fire Department.

Fig. 9-18. If you can get the Tragic Clown painting to catch on fire—say, near a fireplace—the Tragic Clown goes up in smoke, too.

2. Bring the average mood of all Sims in the household up to 25. It's not always easy because the clown wreaks havoc with family mood, making everyone tired and cranky and uncomfortable. But if you can do it, the clown hops in a hole and leaves permanently.

What a Gas! Party Balloons (§50)

This inexpensive decorative item is well worth its cost. A bouquet of party balloons attracts visitors and encourages them to stay longer. First, place the balloons anywhere on the lot. One of the five balloons in the bouquet pops every 50 minutes after placement. Every half-hour after placement, the balloons generate an approximate 50-percent chance of a neighbor drop-in visit. (Be sure your household Sims *greet* visitors to invite them in.) The "visitor generation" continues until either five neighbors visit or the last balloon pops.

Fig. 9-19. Party balloons attract neighbors and keep them around longer.

NOTE

Thankfully, What a Gas! Party Balloons generate no visits between the hours of 12 a.m. and 6 a.m.

But that's not all. Party balloons also cause the Comfort, Hygiene, Bladder, and Hunger motives to decay more slowly, keeping everyone in a better mood for longer. Plus, they cause the Social motive to decay *faster*, which prompts Sims to seek more frequent social interactions with other partygoers to replenish it.

Servo the Home Robot (§15,000)

Any Sim, child or adult, can activate Servo, the expensive but multifunctional time saver from Shiny Things Inc. This experimental robot serves as a replacement for maid, gardening, repair, and even pizza-delivering services. Although the initial cost is steep—§15,000—the long-term savings can be significant because Servo performs all of these services for free. Plus, he entertains guests with digital aplomb.

Servo comes with a docking station that serves as his control center. (You can't interact by clicking on the robot itself.) When you select "Turn On," Servo emerges and immediately begins to function according to the following cycle.

Fig. 9-20. Servo does it all for you—cleaning, cooking, gardening, repair work, even entertaining.

1. Servo looks for anything that needs cleaning, then fulfills the Maid function.

2. Servo looks for anything that needs repair, then fulfills the Repairman function.

3. Servo looks for anything that needs gardening, then fulfills the Gardener function.

4. Finally, Servo scans Sims on the lot for low motive scores.

- If Servo finds low Hunger scores, he serves food. (You can order Servo to serve food manually at the docking station, as well.) Servo's meals provide the same Hunger motive boost as a serving of pizza.

- If Servo finds a Sim with low Social or Comfort scores, he engages the Sim in social activities—entertains, tells jokes, gives back rubs, dances, or talks. (Servo's talk interests are all set to 100 percent; he knows *everything*.)

Servo wears an appropriate hat when performing the aforementioned services. When not in use, Servo reenters the docking station and goes into "Off" mode. He breaks with use and, naturally, is very difficult to repair. Note that you cannot sell Servo unless he is inside his docking station.

Christmas Tree (§199)

Brighten up the Sim Yuletide with this festive addition to the holiday season. Its cheery blinking lights and four wrapped gifts give your Room score a healthy boost. And the gifts are more than just show; Sims can actually open all four. When each gift is opened, it disappears, just like real life.

> **NOTE**
> All outcomes of Servo's social interactions are the same as those of a "person" Sim. Reactions of Sims to Servo's social advances are based on their Outgoing trait. But (of course) there is no Relationship change, because you can't have a "relationship" with a digital/mechanical device. Uh, can you?

Of course, Sims (being almost human) don't always *like* what they get. When a Sim opens a Christmas package, there's a 1 in 5 chance of hating the gift. This lowers the Sim's Fun score by 20 points. Most of the time, however, Sims are pleased by their gifts, which raises Fun by 20 points.

The tree can be placed indoors or outdoors and dies somewhere between five to ten days after placement. A dead tree, of course, drags down Room scores. The only way to dispose of a dead Christmas tree is to delete it in Buy mode.

Fig. 9-21. The lovely Sim Christmas tree has presents for all. Gifts are fun—usually.

Beejaphone Guitar (§580)

Livin' Large adds a new type of musical instrument for Sims to enjoy (or not) in the game. When played, the guitar builds Creativity skill, and the quality of play improves as the Creativity score increases. Playing the Beejaphone always boosts the player's Fun motive and wakes any adult Sim (not kids) asleep in the same room.

Fig. 9-22. The guitar builds Creativity and offers a Fun boost to skilled players and their audience.

Like the piano, the guitar offers a "joinable" activity—that is, you can direct other controllable Sims to "Join," or they may come watch autonomously. (A good player will likely draw an audience.) A Sim playing the guitar advertises Fun and Social increases to everyone, including visitors. Sims who join will watch and offer positive or negative responses based on the skill of the player.

- If the guitar player has a high Creativity skill, watchers gain Fun points and raise their Relationship score toward the player.
- If the guitar player has a low Creativity skill, watchers lower their Relationship score toward the player.

Sky Scorcher Fireworks Kit (§90)

There's nothing like an explosive device to really get your Fun juices flowing. The fireworks kit advertises Fun to Sims at night, but you can use it during the day, too. Rockets shoot into the sky, then fall into an ash pile—unless they hit something. Objects hit by falling fireworks may burst into flames. Note also that any indoor use of the Sky Scorcher *always* ignites a fire.

Fig. 9-23. Fireworks are always fun. Just don't set them off in the house.

Little Voodoo Dolly (§65)

Adult use only. The voodoo doll is one of our favorite new items. Really, what could be more fun than inflicting unspeakable torment on friends and family? When you click on the Little Voodoo Dolly, you get a pie menu of names, like the one you get when using the phone. Your options include everyone in the household plus visiting adult friends. Pick the loved one you want to suffer.

After the choice is made, your Sim either shakes, slaps, or sticks a pin into the doll. The target Sim appears in the PIP window in the corner, suffering a reaction. But wait. The fun's not over yet. If the afflicted Sim is in the same room as the perpetrator, he or she approaches and slaps the nasty voodoo-user. Family dynamics have rarely been this well simulated.

List of Object Interactions

Fig. 9-24. The voodoo doll lets you indulge your dark side, inflicting pain on friends and family.

The objects in the following list appear in the Buy and Build mode catalogs of *The Sims*. Each description includes this useful information when it applies:

- Cost (in simoleans)
- Motives affected by interaction
- Group activity offered
- Breakable/unbreakable
- Adult-only/kid-only
- How object works and/or how best to interact with it

Pay particular attention to the motives each object affects. In general (but not always), the more expensive an object, the more points it boosts the affected motive. For example, expensive chairs are more comfortable; expensive computers are more fun. Check *www.thesims.com* regularly for new objects and other game info.

Alarm: Burglar (§250)

Goes off when a burglar enters the room. Calls police automatically. Keeps blaring until burglar leaves the room. Wakes up sleeping adults and kids in the same room. When placed on the exterior of a house, it detects outside burglar motion within five grid tiles. For more about burglars, see "Fire, Theft, and Accidents" in chapter 7, "Sim Economics 101."

Alarm: Smoke (§50)

Goes off if a fire starts in the same room. Calls Fire Department automatically. Continues ringing until fire is out. Wakes up Sims sleeping in the same room. For more about fire, see "Fire, Theft, and Accidents" in chapter 7, "Sim Economics 101."

Aquarium (§200)

Motives: Fun. Tank gets dirty if not cleaned. Fish die if not fed. Fish die quicker in a dirty tank. There's no cost to feed the fish but it does cost to restock them. Boosts Room score.

Ash Pile

An ash pile appears on the floor after fire destroys an object. Ashes drag down Room score. Can be swept up.

Baby

Motive: Fun (if you choose Play). Yes, babies are "objects" in *The Sims*. Fun objects. Sometimes. For more on babies, see "Family and Housemates" in chapter 5, "Social Interactions."

Bar (§780–§800)

Motives: Fun, Hunger, Bladder (lowers). Two models available. Adult can have a single drink or make multiple drinks for a group of adults; drinks don't cost money. Kids don't make drinks, but can open the bar fridge and take out a can of soda.

Barbecue (§350)

Motive: Hunger. Adults only. Grilling food creates a group meal platter. Can start a fire if a burnable object sits on an adjacent tile, but the BBQ itself won't burn. For more about fire, see "Fire, Theft, and Accidents" in chapter 7, "Sim Economics 101."

Basketball Hoop (§650)

Motives: Fun, Energy (lowers). Group activity. One or two people can play at once. Family member can play alone. Visitors must join a family member to play. (For more on joinable activities, see "Keeping Visitors Happy" in chapter 5, "Social Interactions.") Higher Body skill increases chances of making a basket. Max Fun available varies according to Active trait rating.

Bed (§300–§4,500)

Motives: Energy, Comfort. Seven models available. Once a bed has been slept in, it appears unmade. Unmade beds lower Room scores. Note that more expensive beds fill your Energy needs faster, saving you about an hour of sleep per night. They are also more comfortable. For more on beds, see "Sleeping with Housemates" in chapter 5, "Social Interactions" and "Energy" in chapter 3, "Mood and Motives."

Bills

These arrive in the mailbox every three days. Sims must pay their bills within 10 days or the Repo Man comes and repossesses household items. Color-coded:

- White: Not overdue
- Yellow: Three days overdue
- Orange: Six days overdue
- Red: Nine days overdue

For more about bills, see "Bills and the Repo Man" in chapter 7, "Sim Economics 101."

Bookshelf (§250–§910)

Motive: Fun (for Read, not for Study). Improves Cooking and Repair skills. Four models available. Read Books, Study Cooking or Mechanical, Study for School (kids only). Sim goes to nearest vacant chair and sits to read. If chair is unavailable, Sim reads standing up. Sims must be directed to study. However, Sims (particularly Serious ones) will read a book on their own to raise their Fun scores. All bookshelves give Skill points at the same rate. For more on skill-building activities, see chapter 6, "Careers and Skills."

Chair: Movable (§80–§1,400)

Motive: Comfort. Eleven models available. Sit to relax or engage in seated activity—Watch TV, Play Chess, Eat, Use Computer. Sims may seat themselves from the back and scoot the chair forward to a desk or table.

Chair: Plush (§80–§1,200)

Motive: Comfort. Ten models available, including the "hyper-comfy" Egg Chair. High Comfort. Sims can't scoot plush chairs to tables or desks. More expensive chairs provide more Comfort.

TIP

A good strategy is to sit while doing something else (reading, eating, playing chess, watching TV) to help raise your Comfort motive while building skills or boosting Fun and Hunger scores.

Chair: Recliner (§250–§850)

Motive: Comfort, Energy (Nap). Two models available.

Chessboard (§500)

Motive: Fun. Group activity. Improves Logic skill. (For more on skill-building activities, see chapter 6, "Careers and Skills.") One person can play alone or with a second person. (For more on joinable activities, see "Keeping Visitors Happy" in chapter 5, "Social Interactions.") Max Fun point value varies by personality. Serious types have more fun. But Sims won't get bored if Fun levels are maxed out, because they can play for Logic skill.

Clock: Alarm (§30)

Once set, it rings two hours before car pool arrives for any sleeping Sim in the room. (If the Sim is awake, the alarm won't sound.) However, it awakens everyone in the room regardless of car-pool time. Once set, it functions daily until unset.

Clock: Cuckoo (§180)

Motive: Room. Can be viewed only. Goes cuckoo at 12 a.m., 6 a.m., 12 p.m., and 6 p.m.

Clock: Grandfather (§3,500)

Motive: Room. Adults only. Once wound, runs for 24 hours. When it runs down, it advertises high Room points until it's wound again.

Coffee: Espresso Machine (§450)

Motives: Energy, Fun, Bladder (lowers). Adults only. Drink Espresso. Affords a greater energy boost than regular coffeemaker. Breaks down randomly.

Coffeemaker (§85)

Motives: Energy, Bladder (lowers). Adults only. Less energy boost than espresso machine.

Computer (§999–§6,500)

Motive: Fun. Four models available. Play Games, Get a Job, or Study (kids only). Breaks based on use. The cheaper the computer, the sooner it breaks. (Just like real life!) Only three jobs available each Sim day. Playing computer games awakens sleeping adults in the same room (but not kids).

Counter (§150–§800 per section)

Six models are available—five kitchen, one bathroom. Food Prep, Serving Group Meals, Object Placement. Not an Eating Surface! You may not sell or delete a counter if something sits on it. But if you move the counter, anything on it moves with it.

You may place and use bathroom counters in the kitchen, and kitchen counters in the bathroom. If the kitchen has no counter or food processor, your Sims may use a bathroom counter to prepare food. Counters add Food points, and you need them to prepare most meals. The trick is to keep Sims from leaving things on them! For more on food, see "Hunger: The Food Chain Revealed," in chapter 3, "Mood and Motives."

Fig. 9-25. Counters can round off corners nicely. To create a corner section, place a regular counter at a junction between counters.

Desk (§80–§999)

Four models are available. Used primarily to place objects such as computers, lamps, telephones, and the like. Desks are listed as "desk/table" in the catalog, and can be used as Eating and Serving surfaces. In fact, if you're tight on space, use a desk instead of a table. They fit easier into snug spaces. No Food Prep, though; only counters work for that.

Dishwasher (§550–§950)

Breakable! Two models available. Using the dishwasher is faster than washing dishes in the sink. Placement or Serving Surface, but not Eating Surface. Random breakdowns—cheaper model breaks more often. Floods if used after it's broken.

Dollhouse (§180)

Motive: Fun. Group activity. First person to play always goes to the open side of the dollhouse. Max Fun points varies according to Playful personality rating. For more on joinable activities, see "Keeping Visitors Happy" in chapter 5, "Social Interactions."

Dresser/Armoire (§250–§2,500)

Six models—three dressers, three armoires. Change Clothes. Units never run out of clothes. Adults and kids can use it to change into PJs, swimsuit, or regular clothes. Adults also can change into formal wear or work clothes. Sims can change out of their default clothing using the dresser/armoire, and even change their body type, adding or losing 100 pounds.

Easel (Painting) (§3,500)

Motive: Fun. Improves Creativity skill (adults only). (For more on skill-building activities, see chapter 6, "Careers and Skills.") More than one Sim (one at a time) can work on a painting to completion. A completed painting may be sold. Its value depends on an average of skills of those who painted during its cycle: skill 0 = §0; 5 = §25; 10 = §500. Sims in a bad mood won't paint.

> **NOTE**
>
> In general, characters don't choose to develop skills autonomously. The easel, piano, and guitar are exceptions because they're Fun objects, as well—that is, that is, they attract Sims by "advertising" increases in the Fun score.

Exercise Machine (§700)

Motive: Energy (lowers). Improves Body skill. (For more on skill-building activities, see chapter 6, "Careers and Skills.") When used, awakens all Sims sleeping in the same room.

Fireplace (§600–§3,000)

Light a Fire. Four models available. Fireplaces are placed in Build mode with the Fireplace tool, not purchased from the Buy mode catalog. May be placed anywhere (inside or outside) against a wall. Fireplace burns for two hours and always adds to Room score, but more so while lit. Anything combustible in an adjacent tile will catch fire, but not right away.

Flamingo (§12)

Motive: Fun. May be viewed or, better, kicked. Increases Room score, so it's not totally useless. Quite a bargain at a mere §12.

Food Processor (§220)

Motive: Hunger. Food Prep. Adds more Hunger points to the meal than using a counter; faster, too. Preparer's Cooking skill affects Food Prep duration. For more on food, see "Hunger: The Food Chain Revealed" in chapter 3, "Mood and Motives."

Fountain (§700)

Motives: Fun, Bladder (lowers). Can Play with fountain. Sims who are Shy (low Outgoing) like the fountain most. Adds to Room score.

Flower: Gift

Friends bring flowers periodically, handing them over during greeting. Increases Room score. Gift flowers wilt in two days.

Hot Tub (§6,500)

Motives: Comfort, Fun, Hygiene. Group activity. Breakable. Adults only. Get In, Soak, Talk, Have Fun. If the first person in has Outgoing 7 or above, he or she gets in naked; otherwise, the Sim wears a swimsuit. Joiners follow the first person's example. Sims can have regular conversations as they soak, and won't get out until all hot tub motives are maxed or a motive falls very low. For more on joinable activities, see "Keeping Visitors Happy" in chapter 5, "Social Interactions."

Tips from the Testers

By far the game's best value, the hot tub contributes to three motives—four if there are other Sims in the tub. Hot-tubbing can replace any Fun/Bath interaction. It's a great way to put visiting Sims in a good mood and increase the likelihood of positive social interaction.

It's expensive, but I recommend buying a hot tub right away. Just make sure you have a phone to call the Repairman when it breaks.

—Andrew Blomquist, Tester

Lamp (§25–§1,150)

Breakable (bulb burns out). Twenty-seven models available—twelve floor, seven desk, eight sconce/wall. Lights turn on automatically when the first Sim enters the room, and turn off when the last Sim exits. You can turn lights on and off manually, which overrides the automatic system until 8 a.m. the next day. Anyone can replace a bulb, and it costs nothing; the time it takes, however, depends on Mechanical skill, and there's a random chance of electrocution. (Repairman never gets electrocuted.)

Lamp: Garden (§50–§1,250)

Exterior ground placement. Four models available. Lights turn on automatically at 6 p.m. and off at 2 a.m. They don't break.

Love 'n Haight Lamp (§80)

Motive: Fun. Adds small amount to Room score. Doesn't break.

Medicine Cabinet (§125)

Motive: Hygiene. Improves Charisma skill (adults only). Brush Teeth to raise Hygiene. For more on skill-building activities, see chapter 6, "Careers and Skills."

Mirror (§100–§1,100)

Four models—three wall, one floor. (Wall models include Medicine Cabinet.) Improves Charisma skill (adults only). For more on skill-building activities, see chapter 6, "Careers and Skills."

Newspaper (Free)

Motive: Fun. Read for a small amount of fun, or Look for a Job. Delivered daily; once there are five papers on the property, delivery will stop until one of them is recycled. Offers only one job per day, and as with the computer, Sims in a bad mood won't look for jobs.

Painting (§45–§7,600)

Motive: Fun. Many choices. (Our personal favorite: "Snails with Icicles in Nose.") Boosts Room score. The more expensive, the more points it contributes. Serious Sims get the most Fun. Sim attitude toward certain paintings is predetermined: the same person always likes or dislikes the same painting, even if it's in a neighbor's house. It's not a function of personality, mood, or anything else.

CAUTION

Beware the "Tragic Clown" painting. See the section on the Tragic Clown earlier in this chapter.

NOTE

Painting and sculpture value appreciates and depreciates randomly.

Phone (§50–§75)

Motives: Fun, Energy (lowers). Call neighbors or services; answer for various reasons. See "Calling Neighbors" in chapter 5, "Social Interactions." Phone rings if:

1. Chance-card call offers proposition, always for money. Example: "You just won §100 on KSIM." No calls at night.
2. Prank phone call. Example: "Do you have Prince Albert in a can?"
3. Boss calls to warn Sim about missed work.
4. A Sim has lost their job.
5. Friends are being ignored.
6. Offers the adoption of a child.

Piano (§3,500–§5,399)

Motives: Fun. Two models available. Improves Creativity skill. (For more on skill-building activities, see chapter 6, "Careers and Skills.") Quality of sound (the actual music) improves as skill increases. Playing piano advertises a special "Come and See Me" message to nearby Sims, including visitors. If the player has high Creativity skill, the watcher gains Fun and Relationship points toward the player. If the player has low Creativity skill, the watcher offers a negative response and loses Fun and Relationship points toward the player. Visitors play only if their Creativity is 8 or higher. (For more on join-able activities, see "Keeping Visitors Happy" in chapter 5, "Social Interactions.") When played, a piano can awaken sleeping adults (not kids) in the same room. If a Sim kid is playing, Sim adults will be nice and give a positive response—no matter how good or bad the performance is.

Pinball Machine (§1,800)

Motive: Fun. Group activity. Breakable. Gives a nice Fun boost, but Playful Sims have more fun. Visitor can join only if family member is playing already. (For more on joinable activities, see "Keeping Visitors Happy" in chapter 5, "Social Interactions.") Two players take turns. When played, awakens sleeping adults (not kids) in the same room.

Play Structure (§1,200)

Motive: Fun. Group activity. A great way to keep Sim kids happy and playing together. Max Fun points increased for Active kids. For more on joinable activities, see "Keeping Visitors Happy" in chapter 5, "Social Interactions."

Pool (§75 per tile)

Motive: Fun, Energy. Improves Body skill. Pools are placed in Build mode with the water tool, not purchased from the Buy mode catalog. Needs ladder to exit. For more on skill-building activities, see chapter 6, "Careers and Skills."

Pool: Diving Board (§300)

Motive: Fun. Best way to enter the pool. Diving boards are placed in Build mode with the water tool, not purchased from the Buy mode catalog.

Pool: Ladder (§200)

The only way to exit a pool, a ladder is a must-have. Pool ladders are placed in Build mode with the water tool, not purchased from the Buy mode catalog.

Pool Table (§4,200)

Motive: Fun. Group activity. High Fun boost for one or two Sims. Sim pool players complete one game, and then stop (unless you order them away). For more on joinable activities, see "Keeping Visitors Happy" in chapter 5, "Social Interactions."

Refrigerator (§600–§2,750)

Motive: Hunger. Four models available. Make or Serve Meals, Get Snacks. Launches Food Prep sequence. The type of meal Sims make will depend on what other cooking appliances are available. For more on food, see "Hunger: The Food Chain Revealed" in chapter 3, "Mood and Motives."

Sculpture/Ornament (§12–§15,000)

Motive: Fun. Choices include "Head in Jar Curio" and various wall ornaments such as the "White Rhino Re-enactment." (Our personal favorite: "Large Black Slab.") Boosts Room score. The more expensive, the more points it contributes. Serious Sims get the most Fun. Sim attitude toward each sculpture is predetermined: the same person always likes or dislikes the same sculpture/ornament. Sculpture/ornament value appreciates and depreciates randomly.

Shower (§650)

Motive: Hygiene. Breakable. Gets dirty. It's still usable when it's broken, but the flooded tiles increase. Before disrobing, a Sim will check to see if anyone else is in the room. If so, the Sim determines whether he or she is in love with the person. If all is clear or if the Sim is in love, he or she disrobes and enters the shower. Otherwise, the Sim tries to shoo interlopers away. After a few seconds, if not alone, the Sim will abort the shower. Messy Sims leave puddles when they get out. Neat Sims will get more Hygiene points than Messy Sims. Neat Sims also shower longer.

Sink (§250–§600)

Motive: Hygiene. Breakable. Four models available. Wash Dishes, Wash Hands. Must be placed in counters (except bathroom pedestal sink). Washing dishes at the sink takes longer than using the dishwasher. If there's no kitchen sink or dishwasher, Sims may wash dishes at a bathroom sink. Neat Sims wash hands automatically after eating pizza or using the toilet if there is a sink available.

Sofa/Loveseat (§150–§2,000)

Motives: Comfort, Energy (Nap). Seven loveseats, nine sofas, one wood settee, and one garden bench available. Sit or Nap. (Can't nap on garden bench.) Expensive sofas, loveseats, and the wood settee add to Room score.

Stereo/Jukebox (§100–§2,550)

Motive: Fun. Group activity (Dance). Two stereo models, a jukebox, and a boom box available. Turn On for music; Dance Alone or with Partner. (Kids always dance alone.) Expense contributes to fun. When it's on, it awakens sleeping adults in the same room (but not kids). Outgoing Sims dance first. Shy Sims are less likely to Join Dance. (For more on joinable activities, see "Keeping Visitors Happy" in chapter 5, "Social Interactions.") One particularly cool feature of the stereo is that you can change the songs played on it by dragging and dropping actual MP3 files into the Music/Stations/ directory.

> NOTE
>
> With each Sim who comes to dance, the lure of the stereo grows stronger. If many Sims are in the household, a dancing crowd often forms in the room with the stereo.

Stove (§100–§1,600)

Three range-top models, one expensive cooktop, two small ovens. Sims use stoves to cook prepared meals, but only after you direct them to the refrigerator. Can start fires, depending on user's Cooking skill. Microwave doesn't start fires. Toaster oven more likely to flame than other stoves. (See the "Fire, Theft, and Accident" section in chapter 7, "Sim Economics 101.") For more details on food and cooking appliances, see "Hunger: The Food Chain Revealed," in chapter 3, "Mood and Motives."

Table: End (§40–§399)

Eight models (including kids' nightstand) available. Place Objects, Serving Surface, but not Food Prep or Eating. Three most expensive models boost Room score.

Toilet (§300–§1,200)

Motive: Bladder! Also lowers Hygiene. Gets dirty. Expensive model boosts Comfort. Breakable (gets clogged). Three models available. Use to you-know-what. Neat Sims are more likely to flush after use. If Bladder score drops below –95, Sims run to the toilet. Clogging is based on how much was deposited since last flush. Anyone can unclog the toilet, but Sims with high repair skill do it more quickly. Flush Force 5 XLT never clogs because it automatically flushes. It also adds to the Room score, as does the new In-house Outhouse model.

Tombstone/Urn

Motive: Social (lowers). Shows up automatically after a Sim dies. Can't be purchased, but may be moved or sold. If a Sim dies outdoors or an urn is moved outdoors, it appears as a tombstone. (Tombstone must be on level ground.) If a Sim dies indoors or a tombstone is moved indoors, it appears as an urn. Each midnight, there's a small probability that an urn or tombstone will generate a Sim ghost. When an urn or tombstone is sold, it no longer generates a ghost.

NOTE
Mourn lowers the Social motive score; Sims seek other Sims for consolation. Don't be surprised if sometimes this consolation comes in strange forms (such as a joke or tickle). Sims have no concept of social appropriateness.

A tombstone/urn advertises the Mourn interaction very highly during the first 24 Sim-hours after a death, so family Sims will grieve autonomously at the burial site. The lure decreases over the next 48 hours. Visitors may mourn during the first 72 hours, too. After that, family Sims can mourn, but only if you direct them to do so. For more on death, see "Death" in chapter 3, "Mood and Motives."

Toy Box (§54)

Motive: Fun. Kids only. Play with the toys it contains for a Fun boost. Only one kid at a time can interact with toy box, picking a random toy each time—car, doll, plane, teddy bear.

Train Set: Large (§955)

Motive: Fun. Group activity. Up to 10 Sims can participate! (For more on joinable activities, see "Keeping Visitors Happy" in chapter 5, "Social Interactions.") One Sim runs the train from the control station. Other Sims grow attracted and come to watch. The more Sims observers gather, the stronger the interaction advertises, drawing even more Sims. This continues until the controller satisfies his or her Fun motive. Then the group disbands. Also boosts Room score.

Train Set: Small (§80)

Motive: Fun. Group activity. Kids only. For more on joinable activities, see "Keeping Visitors Happy" in chapter 5, "Social Interactions."

Trash Can: Inside (§30–§45)

Two models available, including the new "Dungeon Dumpster" trash barrel. Throw trash or ash piles into this receptacle. It fills up after about five deposits. Then you must empty it before you can use it again. (It fills faster than a trash compactor.) Flies appear when the can/barrel is full for six hours.

> **NOTE**
> A full trash can has a negative depreciated value: that is, it detracts from your net worth, Room score, and costs you money if you just delete it.

Trash Can: Outside

Comes with the lot. This can is a bottomless pit. You can't fill it up. You can't move or delete it unless you use the "map_edit on" cheat to unlock the floor tile it sits on, and then use the "move_objects on" cheat. (See chapter 1, "Cheats and Quick Start Tips.")

Trash Compactor (§375)

When full, its drawer opens and the green light turns red. When you select Empty Trash, your Sim pulls out the compactor's bag and takes it to the outside trash can. Serves as Placement, Food Prep, or Serving Surface, but not an Eating Surface. Holds four times as much trash as the indoor trash can.

Trash Pile

When full, has a negative impact on Room score. Appears when trash-bearing Sims find the indoor trash can full or unavailable, or when Messy Sims toss down used snack containers. Clean Up to pick up the pile (it becomes a trash bag) and dump it in nearest trash can.

Tub (§800–§3,200)

Motives: Hygiene, Comfort. Four models available. Sims soak until they get maximum Hygiene score. It gets dirty based on use. Messy people leave a puddle from time to time.

TV (§85–§3,500)

Motive: Fun. Group activity. Breakable. Three models available. Breaks with use, not age. If on, it awakens sleeping adults in the same room (but not kids). Three things modify TV enjoyment:

1. Expensive models provide higher Fun value.
2. Lazy people get more Fun points from watching.
3. Personality types get more Fun points from their preferred channels. Preferences are:
   - Outgoing: Romance
   - Active: Action
   - Playful: Cartoon
   - Grouchy (low Nice): Horror

A Sim may get electrocuted when attempting to repair a broken TV. It depends on Mechanical skill:

TV Repair Hazard

Mechanical Skill Points	Percent Chance of Electrocution
0	100
1	25
2	10
3–10	1

VR Glasses (§2,300)

Motive: Fun. Select Play to wear. Big fun! Only one person at a time may use this. Playful Sims get the most Fun points.

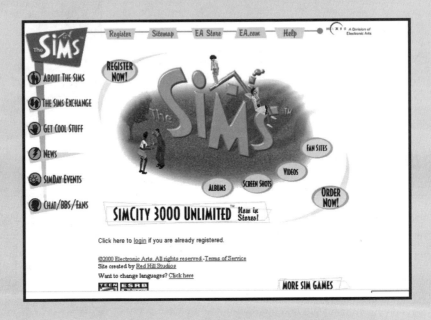

10

How to Find and Create New Sim Stuff

One of the coolest things about *The Sims* and its *Livin' Large* expansion pack is the way you can customize walls, floors, roofs, faces, "skins" (i.e. body textures, including clothes), and even the game's music to reflect your own unique style. You can do the work yourself, using a set of Maxis-created software tools and, in most cases, a software paint program. Or you can download the finished work of others. Either way, it's remarkably easy to put a personal design stamp on your Sim Neighborhoods.

This final chapter gives you a quick overview of how you can customize Sims stuff and trade it with other players. First, we'll show you how to find everything you need. Then we'll take a look at the three primary customization tools: *FaceLift*, *HomeCrafter*, and *SimShow*. Note that each tool comes with a detailed tutorial that you can view with your browser.

Where to Find New Sim Stuff

You can find all kinds of user-created Sim skins, faces, walls, and floors on the Internet. But your first stop for new Sim paraphernalia should always be the official EA/Maxis website for *The Sims*, located at *http://www.thesims.com*.

There you'll find plenty of official info about the game, plus links to other Sims-related sites. Look for new Maxis-created objects (see the Slot Machine in figure 10-12) and check out The Sims Exchange, a library where you can upload your Sim folks, houses, and family albums, and download the same from other players.

You can also find many fan sites devoted to *The Sims* on the Internet. One of the best as of this writing is Steve Bonham's "The Sims Resource" at *http://www.thesimsresource.com*. Two other good ones are "Mall of The Sims" at *http://www.mallofthesims.com* and "Simz Online" at *http://www.simzonline.com*.

Keep in mind that Internet sites

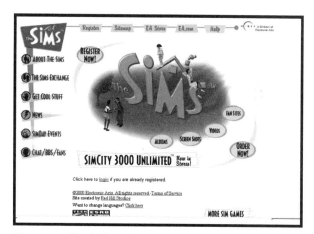

Fig. 10-1. Check the official Maxis website for updates, new objects, and links to other fun sites devoted to THE SIMS.

are often fluid entities. By the time you read this, the ones we've listed here may no longer exist. But trust us, you can find lots of good stuff out there. Even the laziest search engine should locate dozens (if not hundreds) of sites.

Fig. 10-2. Sims-related fan sites like these flourish on the Internet.

Where to Put New Sim Stuff

Once you create or download a new object, skin, or texture file, you must put it in the proper game folder before you can use it in *The Sims*. Here's where to save new stuff:

- Head and body textures in *The Sims*\GameData\Skins
- Floors in *The Sims*\GameData\Floors
- Walls in *The Sims*\GameData\Walls
- Roofs in *The Sims*\GameData\Roofs

How to Add New Stuff: Getting Started

Before you can start customizing *The Sims* into your own personal playground, you need tools. Fortunately, these tools are easy to find and pop into your virtual tool belt.

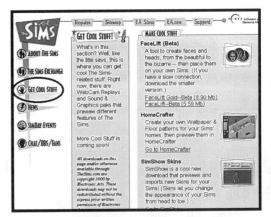

Fig. 10-3. To find customization tools, click the "Get Cool Stuff" button on the main screen of the official EA/Maxis website for THE SIMS.

Downloading THE SIMS Utilities

The first things you need are the three utility programs: *HomeCrafter* for viewing new wall and floor tiles, *FaceLift* for creating new Sim heads, and *SimShow* for viewing new Sim body skins. Go to the official EA/Maxis website for *The Sims* at *http://www.thesims.com*. Then click on the Get Cool Stuff button. From there, you can find and download the *FaceLift*, *HomeCrafter*, and *SimShow* tools.

The Difference Between Mesh and Skin

Before we go any further, let's discuss the difference between "mesh" and "skin." A skin is the colorful surface texture of a Sim—the face, skin, hair, and clothes. This texture is applied or "wrapped" around a mesh. Each mesh is a full 3D shape, body and/or head, underneath the skin—a kind of blank wire-frame space that the skin gets layered over.

You cannot edit body meshes with any Sim tool. In fact, both *SimShow* and *HomeCrafter* are merely preview tools that let you view skin or wall/floor textures

Fig. 10-4. A "skin" is the colored texture that wraps around a "mesh," or body/head shape. Here's the body skin of a Sim female in shorts and the head skin of a Sim female brunette.

previously created or edited with a software paint program. However, you *can* change head shapes and create new mesh/skin combinations with the awesome *FaceLift* tool. In *FaceLift* you're creating actual head/face files; in *HomeCrafter* and *SimShow*, you're only viewing files previously created by either you or someone else.

All three tools let you export the files directly into *The Sims* for use in the game.

FaceLift

This tool is a blast! Accessible for all users, *FaceLift* allows you to design new heads for characters in *The Sims* by morphing the shape and skin of preset heads. Warning: Making heads can be addictive! This free utility is so fun and easy-to-use, you'll spend hours making your Sims movie stars and freaks.

Fig. 10-5. The FACELIFT tool

Fig. 10-6. FACELIFT tools let you "fine tune" the eye, nose, and mouth/jaw areas of each face. Here's the same face twice—one with all features set narrow, the other with all set wide.

You'll begin with nine randomly-generated heads. Choose the head that is closest to the one you want. You can now specify how different or similar to that head you want the next set of heads to be. For example, you can focus on changing hairstyle while leaving the face the same. Or, you can focus on skin color while leaving the shape of the head alone. Once you've gotten close to what you're going for, tweak the face with *FaceLift*'s Fine Tune feature and give it a description, gender, age, and skin color. Once you've finished, *FaceLift* lets you export the new head directly into your game folder with the appropriate filename code. And don't worry if you don't like the finished product—you can get a new set of nine heads any time you like!

HomeCrafter

HomeCrafter allows you to preview floor and wall patterns to see how they will look in the game, then export them directly into *The Sims*. Note that this utility doesn't help you create the patterns. Instead, it loads existing images and converts them for use in the game.

Fig. 10-7. The HOMECRAFTER tool

So to create your own custom floor/wall tiles, start by using a software paint program (*Photoshop* or *Paint Shop Pro* are good examples) to create patterns and save them as *.bmp* or *.jpg* files. Or, if art isn't your thing, you can use images created by anyone or anything. *HomeCrafter* can load any *.bmp* or *.jpg* image file in your system, even photo image files. Imagine wallpapering a haunted Sim house with repeating images of Britney Spears. What a chilling thought! For the best results, make your images the size specified in the tutorial. Otherwise, the game will stretch them to suit its needs.

Fig. 10-8. The HOMECRAFTER screen consists of a control panel, a sample room to preview your custom wall/floor tiles, and the text description box on the bottom.

TIP

Here's a mini-cheat. Use *HomeCrafter* to save big on decorating costs. Both wall and floor tiles can be priced at as low as §1, then imported into the game. This lets you install coverings at a fraction of the normal cost.

Once you have the *.bmp* or *.jpg* images, load them into *HomeCrafter* (which automatically converts the images into either wall or floor tiles) and place them in the sample room. You can enter descriptions that actually appear in the game, and set the price per tile, as well. Finally, you can export them directly into *The Sims*. *HomeCrafter* automatically places wall/floor tiles in the correct game folder with necessary game info.

SimShow

SimShow lets you preview new Sim body/head skins and export them into your game. As with *HomeCrafter*, you don't actually create files in *SimShow*. Instead, you view existing Sims—that is, Sims with skin textures applied to mesh bodies. The skins, however, may be ones you've edited with an external paint program (like *Photoshop* or *Paint Shop Pro*). Thus, *SimShow* gives you a way to preview your work. Or the skins you view may be downloaded from a friend or fan site.

> **NOTE**
> Refer back to figure 10-4 to see the kinds of body and head textures you can edit. then view on Sims to create new skins for your game.

In any case, *SimShow* is a fabulous viewing tool. And once you see a Sim you like, whether created by you or by someone else, *SimShow* lets you easily put the creation into

The Sims by automatically exporting the images to the appropriate in-game folders and formats. The new Sim then becomes available in the game's Create a Sim screen.

Fig. 10-9. SIMSHOW lets you view Sim characters and their animations both before and after you edit their textures.

> **NOTE**
> Getting a skin to wrap properly around a "mesh" (3D body shape) can be tricky. To learn more about editing skins, consult Maxis Assistant Producer Sean Baity's guide, included when you download SimShow. There's a detailed, step-by-step tutorial in which Baity puts his own face and clothes on a Sim body shape. You can also find an excellent tutorial entitled "Skinning 101" and a skin database in the Simz Online website at http://simz.gamenation.com/features/skinning.

Other Drop-In Assets

The Sims also lets you drop your own music into the game.

MP3 Music Files

You can add MP3-format music files into game folders to person-alize the music that plays in the background or on the in-game stereos. Note: You can't change the names of the in-game radio stations, just what music plays when you select a station.

Here's where to place MP3s so they play on the station you want:

- Put Country station music in the Music\Stations\Country directory.
- Put Classical station music in the Music\Stations\Classica directory.
- Put Latin station music in the Music\Stations\Latin directory.
- Put Rock station music in the Music\Stations\Rock directory.
- Put Build Mode background music in the Music\Modes\Build directory.
- Put Buy Mode background music in the Music\Modes\Buy directory.
- Put Neighborhood background music in the Music\Modes\NhoodUS directory (in the U.S.-elsewhere, use the Nhood directory).

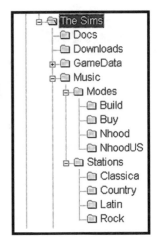

Fig. 10-10. Put your own MP3 files into the appropriate folders within the THE SIMS Music directory to get new music to play in the background or on the in-game radio stations.

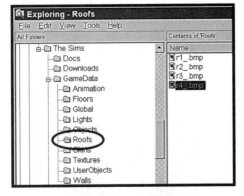

Fig. 10-11. Put your .BMP roof patterns in this directory. Make sure they're the right size and pixel depth.

Roof Patterns

You can add new roof textures to *The Sims*, too. First, create and save a pattern as a 256-color *.bmp* file, 32-by-32 pixels in size with a pixel depth of 8. Then drop the file into the Gamedata\Roofs folder (see Figure 10-11).

Objects

Over time, Maxis will release more objects for your down-loading pleasure. To get them, simply go to the official website. Each new object will include auto-installers that automatically put all the files associated with the object into the appropriate directories. The first new object (available 2/4/2000) was a slot machine. Objects that followed included a moose head, a pet guinea pig in a cage, and wall sconces. (*Livin' Large* includes all of these new objects posted by Maxis, up to the release of the expansion pack.)

DOWNLOADS FOR YOUR GAME

Game Downloads!

It is just the beginning! We are busy brainstorming and creating more fun objects for you. All objects, homes and skins in this section are for your game! We currently have 5 new houses for your game and a Slot Machine for your Sims to play. Downloads for your Game

Fig. 10-12. The first new object download available at THE SIMS official website was the venerable slot machine. Hey, what's a home without one?

NOTE

The downloadable slot machine is a money cheat. If your Fun motive is low, your odds of winning simoleans are very high.

Creating New Objects with the SimTransmogrifier

The SimTransmogrifier is a tool that lets you clone objects that already exist in *The Sims*, then edit the text of the catalog description, change the price, or edit the catalog icon and popup images. You can also export an object's graphics as .bmp files, edit them with a paint program like *Photoshop* or *Paint Shop Pro*, then import them back into the game.

Does that sound fun, or what? For example: You can make a pink lawn flamingo into a green one and change its description into experimental fiction. In fact, you'll find this very example (and the wickedly hilarious new catalog text) at the website listed below. To download SimTransmogrifier and complete documentation on how to use the tool, go to *www.lushcreations.com/SimTools/SimTransmogrifier*.

Sharing Families

As *The Sims* manual points out, if you've checked the Export HTML option in the Play Options for the game, important .jpg shots of family members (w/statistics), family houses, and house information is saved (by house address) in the Web Pages folder of the *Sims* directory. It happens automatically—you can delete them if you don't want them or edit them in an image-editing program.

This awesome web publishing tool lets you post each Sim family's web page online in The Sims Exchange and look for other families to download into your neighborhood. To find the Sims Exchange, go to *www.thesims.com*, then have a blast finding and down-loading other people's houses. Your in-game photo album is posted online for other users to read, too. With the photo captions, it's like creating a storybook. Build your family stories day to day, then share them with others. To view your own family's web page, click the View with Web Pages button on the game's neighborhood screen.

New Web Page Templates

New and improved web page templates are included in the *Livin' Large* expansion pack. These make it easier to view web page albums posted to The Sims Exchange. Previously created family albums will be preserved, but new easy-to-view thumbnails are generated automatically. The old web page templates will be renamed and moved to the backup folder UserData\Old Web Templates. You can delete this directory if you have never modified your original web templates.

Improved Family Importing in LIVIN' LARGE

You'll also notice a new button on the neighborhood screen that looks like a house with a plus sign. This is the new Import Family button. Instead of automatically prompting you to import a family as soon as it's in the import folder, *Livin' Large* now gives you the option to import families *you* want into the neighborhood *you* specify.

Simply switch to your desired neighborhood with the neighborhood arrow buttons in the screen's upper left corner. Then click the Import Family button to import your downloaded households. A dialog box will appear, prompting you to import the families you have downloaded.

This button will only function if you have a family to import in your UserData\Import folder. When you download houses from The Sims Exchange, they automatically go into this Import folder. Likewise, when you save a household, it appears in the UserData\Export folder, ready for upload to The Sims Exchange if you wish. Again, these are automatic functions that the player does not need to manage.

Fig. 10-13. After downloading a family from The Sims Exchange (using The Sims Teleportation System) into the UserData\Import folder, just switch to the neighborhood you want and hit Import Family.

> **NOTE**
> As of this writing, foreign language versions of The Sims: Livin' Large will not have the ability to upload or download families.

C

Call Here interaction, 75

candy, 30

car pool, 101, 102, 104–109

career "chance" cards, 101

career tracks

    choosing, 96–97

    list of, 96

    and motive decay, 100–101

    personality traits required for specific, 97

    and promotion opportunities, 96, 99

    and skill-building, 99

    skills required for specific, 97

    table of requirements/positions, 104–109

Casino, 146

catalog

    Build mode, 161

    Buy mode, 23, 36, 144, 161

chairs

    catalog description, 163–164

    and Comfort motive, 32

    interactions/ad value, 54

    and Room score, 38

"chance" cards, career, 101

Change Clothes, 121

Charisma skill, 17, 103

chartreuse potion, 148

cheat codes, 2–5, 6–7, 18, 134, 135, 183

Cheat window, opening, 2

Cheer Up interaction, 75, 76

Chemistry Lab, 19, 32, 83

chemistry set, 55

chess, 55

chessboard, 52, 164

children. *See* babies; kids.

Chin, Eric, vi

Christmas tree, 38, 159

CiaoTime cooktop, 26

cleanup, after-meal, 30–31

clock, 38, 55, 164

clothes, 121

clown. *See* Tragic Clown.

cockroaches. *See* roaches.

coffeemaker, 55, 164, 165

color bars, motive, 21

columns, support, 138, 141

"Come and See Me" message, 143

Comfort motive

    decay of, 23

    and furniture, 31–32

    and Little Voodoo Dolly, 32

    weighting of, 22–23

communication, iv

compactor, trash, 31, 36, 39, 63, 174

Compliment interaction, 75, 76

computer, 37, 38, 51, 55, 165

"Concatenation Station" Home Chemistry
    Lab, 19, 32, 83, 147–149

construction. *See* Build mode.

contribution curve, happiness, 47–49

conversation

    how it works, 70–73

    mapping, 67

    during other activities, 71–72

    scoring, 71

    starting, 70, 71

    topics/icons, 67–70

cooking appliances, 25–27

cooking fire, 128

PRIMAGAMES.COM

More Than Just Strategy

Strategy:

Over 250 Fast Track Guides with many more to come — new online strategy every week.

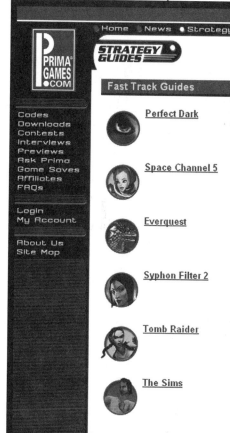

Perfect Dark

Space Channel 5

Everquest

Syphon Filter 2

Tomb Raider

The Sims

News:

A daily digest of game industry news — our news area is the best place to start if you want to know what's new in games.

Game Worlds:

Our Game Worlds are dedicated to the most popular games and supported by our wealth of Fan Site Affiliates.

www.primagames.com

Home
News
Strategy Guides
Forums
Game Worlds

Strategy